ENDORSEM.

"I loved her voice. She's one of the really fine singers of our era."

The late music producer **Jerry Wexler** (Aretha Franklin, Bob Dylan, Willie Nelson, Donny Hathaway)

"She sounded like she was crying, her voice was crying. She's got a pleading sound to her voice, and that's what attracted me to her voice. She's always been one of my favorite singers. There ain't no question about that."

Kenny Gamble (Legendary composer and founder of Philadelphia International Records which birthed the Philly Soul Sound of the 1970s.)

"Candi is a soft-hearted person who's led a thrilling but hard life. Back in the `70s, she drank hard, partied hard, loved hard, and she endured a lot of hard knocks as a woman in a man's music business. All of that hardness toughened her self-preservation and transformed her into the victorious survivor she has now become."

Bill Carpenter (Publicist for Candi Staton)

HERITAGE BUILDERS

PUBLISHING

Young Hearts Run Free

First Lady of Southern Soul

HERITAGE BUILDERS PUBLISHING
MONTEREY CALIFORNIA

HERITAGE BUILDERS PUBLISHING

First Edition 2016

Co-Writer and Editor Dr. Sherman Smith
Cover Design Rae House
Book Design Keith Bennett
Published by Heritage Builders Publishing
Monterey, California 93940
www.HeritageBuildersPublishing.com
1-800-397-8267

ISBN 978-1-942603-58-0

PRINTED AND BOUND IN THE
UNITED STATES OF AMERICA

HERITAGE BUILDERS
PUBLISHING

PREFACE

It was Saturday morning, and I can still smell the bacon and cinnamon rolls cooking on the stove. The succulent smell filled the air that summer morning in every room of the small house where we lived.

A couple closely related to us on my mother's side of the family would come often from Birmingham to help us. They helped my mother support us by bringing groceries and clothing for us girls. I really loved them.

When we would see the car coming down the dusty road, we would run out to meet them. The husband was a tall man and would always pick me up, toss me in the air, and then kiss me on the neck. I just loved him because he was so much fun to be around.

This particular morning, his wife was helping my mama cook our breakfast. My two sisters and I were horsing around with him. We loved to wrestle with him when he was with us for the weekends, so we were down rolling on the floor.

My oldest sisters were fourteen and eleven years old. I was nine years old. We were playing, laughing, and having so much fun. All of a sudden, his countenance changed.

"I'm tired," he said. "You all go on out and play. Go on now."

"Not you," he said to me as he grabbed my hand. "You stay in here with me."

He got back in bed, and then pulled me in with him. He immediately started fondling me. He began touching me with his private part until he was satisfied.

"Now get up and go wash," he instructed me. "Put on a clean dress, and don't you ever tell anyone about this. It's our little secret, okay?"

"Yes sir," I replied.

I walked out totally confused, but I knew I had been violated. I didn't know how to deal with what happened to me. I felt so shattered and broken, but I did as I was instructed. I went outside and sat on the front steps of our house. I was deep in thought about what happened when my mama announced that breakfast was ready.

I went into the kitchen and tried to act normal, but I couldn't do it. I could not look at him. I felt terribly guilty; even though, I knew I had done nothing wrong. I couldn't face his wife. I didn't look at her.

I ate my breakfast, and then went out to play with my sisters. I never, ever mentioned anything to them about the violation, and my mother never knew what he did to me.

Many young boys and girls go through this, and what they don't tell, they act out. This was the beginning of my downward spiral trying to maintain a normal relationship. I couldn't be in a relationship with a good man with excellent character and morals. I always ended up with men that abused me, and I made so many wrong choices.

I kept my secret until I was fifty years old – more than forty-one years. I kept it filed away in my tightly guarded mental safety deposit box. I started shrinking backwards. I wanted to forget, so I thought drugs would be the answer not realizing the seeds of molestation had taken root and destroyed my perception.

If you've been molested, please tell somebody. It is one of the major reasons I am writing this book. Perhaps it will change your thinking, so that you will have the courage to expose the person who hurt you.

God Bless,
Candi Staton

ACKNOWLEDGEMENTS

I want to thank God for allowing me to write this book and to be able to remember my story. I thank Him that I am still here to tell it.

I want to thank my children for being patient and loving during my times of uncertainties and distress.

I want to thank my sons, Marcel Williams, Marcus Williams, Terry Williams, Clarence Carter, Jr, and Cassandra Hightower, and their families for being there for me whenever I needed them.

I want to thank my eighteen grandchildren and my ten great-grandchildren for their love and support.

A very special thanks to my publicist for over thirty years, Bill

Carpenter. If I needed to know anything about my history, I would just call Bill. I don't know what I would have done without him. Thank you Bill.

I want to thank my sister, Maggie Staton Peebles, for her wisdom and advice.

I want to thank my husband, Henry Hooper, who has been my stabilizing factor. I love you, honey.

I want to thank Pastor Kenneth Whalum and his wife, Sheila, for their fervent prayers on my behalf.

I want to thank Dr. Sherm Smith and Heritage Builders Publishing for believing in this project and for the untiring commitment to make the book a reality.

FOREWARD

by Dr. Sherman Smith

There are singers that some of us follow for a lifetime, and there are famous singers that none of us ever follow, and we don't know much about them until they somehow cross our paths.

This was not the case with Candi Staton and me. I followed Candi's career off and on and loved her beautiful soulful voice as I do to this day. I never dreamed I would ever meet her much less publish a book about her memoirs.

I published a book on Rick Hall of Fame Studios located in Muscle Shoals, Alabama. *Rick Hall, The Man From Muscle Shoals, My Journey from Shame to Fame* was where I learned that Rick was and probably still is the number one music producer in the world.

Rick Hall recorded many hit songs on Candi Staton, and it was during the production of his memoirs that I learned all about this person whose captivating voice had entertained me most of my life.

CBS Nightly News was filming a segment at Fame Studios and wanted a singer that Rick had produced, and who was famously at the top of the world of music. Candi Staton got the call.

When the filming was completed, I was standing alone, and Candi was in a conversation with Linda Hall, Rick's wife.

"I am writing a book," Candi explained, "and I need a publisher."

Linda looked at me, but Candi couldn't see me. "I know one," Linda said. "Sherm is here."

"Do you think I could talk to him?" Candi asked.

I walked up to Candi and put my arm around her. She looked at me with amazement that this stranger had approached her.

"So, you need a publisher," I said.

Candi nodded affirming that was true. "I'm Sherm," I commented. "You now have a publisher."

Candi's eyes welled with tears, and she exclaimed loudly, "Are you serious!"

"I am," I answered. Candi hugged me and danced. The deal was struck, and this is the fascinating story of a talented lady that was born in poverty in southern Alabama and became a big star.

Not long after we began our journey, I was in New Orleans working on another story. I was driving around in the rain with Joe Gildersleeve, who I had just met, and Joe was showing me all over New Orleans. Suddenly, my phone rang, and on the screen appeared the name, Candi Staton.

Joe looked at me and mouthed, "Is that the Candi Staton?"

I immediately affirmed that it was indeed the lady, and Joe almost came out of his seat.

"I've been a fan all my life. She's my favorite singer!"

"Would you like to talk with her?" I asked.

"Would I? Can I?" Joe shouted.

Candi Staton was so gracious. She talked to a fan she never knew idolized her, and Joe was beside himself that she would take the time to talk to him.

I have been with Candi for hours on end. I have visited her home many times while working on this book. I know her family, Marcus, Marcel, Terry, Clarence Carter, Jr. and Cassandra, who are her children. This is one of the great families in America in my opinion.

The inspiration I have received from this lady is beyond words. It will be difficult for the reader to comprehend how such a talented person almost from birth could be so mistreated. Yet, Candi, a small woman in stature but a giant in heart, faced every obstacle with unwavering enthusiasm and resolve to beat the Devil out of the Devil.

Young Hearts Run Free was an amazing hit song, and *Young Hearts Run Free* is a book just as amazing. Candi Staton truly is the First Lady of Southern Soul.

INTRODUCTION
by Candi Staton

When you are walking down the road of life, you need to have goals. You must keep focused on those goals because life is full of many distractions. Distraction is your greatest enemy.

I mean no harm, but there are people in your life that won't agree with what you are doing, or where you are going. They will pressure you to change your course and take another path. It is at this point, that you may lose your focus.

It is paramount that you understand that the road you travel may be slower than you have patience to endure. It may be rocky and have twists and turns that hurt your feet, and your back may go out on you.

When this happens, stop and rest awhile and refocus. Before you reach out and hold on to something or someone, make sure they are strong enough to hold you and have the ability to support you.

An old Chinese Proverb says it so well, "The glory is not in ever failing but rising up every time you fail."

I made a major choice that helped me through every crisis in my life. Regardless of what I had been through, I chose joy over sorrow, love over hate, and courage over fear. I chose to live and be happy.

I have made mistakes caused by senseless decisions and bad choices, but I chose to keep hanging on and counted every one of those setbacks as stepping-stones. Through it all, I chose to keep a positive attitude.

I am convinced that happiness in life consists of ten percent of what happens to you, and ninety percent of how you react to it. You can't let negative circumstances of life get you down. You have to walk over them and teach others that life is not about giving up but getting up and moving on.

I have learned that *you can't drown in water until the water gets in you.* As long as you are in a mess, you can live in it; just don't let the mess live in you. That's when you release poisonous words that will kill the spirit in you.

I hope my story will help you make better choices. Don't judge me because you don't know where I've been physically, mentally, or emotionally when I was going through all those tough times.

God was with me every step of the way, and through the guidance of Psalm 91, I've made it this far, and so can you. I could be the poster child for domestic violence. Look at me, check me out. I am a woman, and most look at me as a successful woman. They are right. I am.

I have persevered through many battles. As you read my book, you will come to understand the Spirit behind the horrible cowardly demons that are hiding behind the cloak painted with fear. This demon robs and steals your self-esteem. He's a big bully who keeps pouncing you in your mind, soul, and spirit until there is no more of you left that is recognizable.

He controls your mind, will, and emotions. You can't even think your own thoughts anymore. You're only allowed to think what he allows you to think. How sad to see a free-spirited young woman turned into a caterpillar instead of a butterfly. She is crawling on her belly to do everything she can to please this insensitive monster.

The more obedient and humble she becomes, the more aggressive and insensitive he becomes. There is nothing, absolutely nothing you can do to stop him except escape. It is the only exit for most of these abusive cases. Some don't live to escape, and some do. Some get the courage through the Grace of God to survive.

I write about these things because I have experienced and walked through them. You have to live it to know it.

Candi Staton

Young Hearts Run Free

First Lady of Southern Soul

CHAPTER ONE

You've Got the Love I Need to See Me Through

I am so blessed to have a beautiful life, even though I have endured more hardships than most people would ever want in a lifetime. My life has been colorful, and I have been blessed.

I was born in Hanceville, Alabama in the 1940's. I was born a normal, healthy, and strong baby girl weighing nine pounds. My mother said I was a very cute little baby girl and full of life. She would say that my attitude was as if I was expecting the very best God had to offer me.

I was blessed to have a good mother and father although my dad was riddled with problems at times. They had nine children and lost three of them at birth. My oldest sister died when she was nine years old. My siblings were Sam, Joe, Lillie, Maggie, and Robert. This was the family I grew up with living in rural Alabama.

We lived in a small community where the roads were all paved with dirt. It's hard to imagine today living on a dirt road. We used to sit on the front porch and when cars would drive by, we couldn't see for a while until the dust boiling from beneath those tires faded away. Dust was all over the place, and the faster the cars flew by, the worse the dirt and dust. We took it all in stride and fanned the dust away. Eventually, the roads became paved with blacktop, and today it is a beautiful little community.

We were a normal family. Normal back then meant that we were very poor just like every other family eking out a living on those farms. We moved from farm to farm until one day my grandmother, Lula, on my mother's side gave us some land to build a little house on.

Every family struggled and worked hard to earn a living. We raised our own food including corn, beans, greens, potatoes, onions, and peanuts. We raised enough food to carry us through an entire year. We also raised cotton, and every one of us worked in the fields doing the hard labor it took to make ends meet.

My daddy was always there. We had a couple old mules, and daddy was always up early in the morning plowing with those mules. He loved to open up the earth, so that we could plant the crops. In the wintertime when it was too cold for anything to grow, my daddy worked in the coalmines.

On the acreage my grandmother gave us, my mother supervised the building of our first home. The house cost one hundred dollars to build. Mr. Henry was the man who framed up the little house, and we were so proud. It had a tin roof, and we thought we were in heaven.

My daddy finished the inside of the house. We didn't have sheetrock, so wood was used to trim it out. My mother actually put wallpaper over the wood trim, and we had a wonderful home for our family. We had no television, but we did have a radio. There were lots of things going on in the house, and we always kept company with each other.

My mother was a seamstress and was very skilled at her craft. We lived about fifteen miles from the general store that serviced the folks living in the vicinity. My mother always wanted to be at the store when it opened, so we would have to get up at four o'clock in the morning in order to get there when the stores opened.

We traveled in a wagon that my daddy hitched up to his mules. On cold mornings, us kids would crawl in the wagon bed and cover up with quilts in order to stay warm.

My parents would buy enough food and necessary things for the house to last quite a while. My mother would buy one hundred pound sacks of flour, so we would have enough meal, and she also bought large sacks of rice. These sacks were big enough that she would pour the flour into aluminum cans, and then use the sacks to make little dresses for us girls. All the flour sacks were of different patterns and pretty colors and designs, and she made some really nice clothes for us.

My mom would wash the flour sacks after she had emptied them. She would also buy regular material for dresses, but some of these flour sacks had absolutely beautiful floral patterns and were very attractive. We didn't mind wearing flour sacks at all, and we loved the little dresses.

We were happy because our mother taught us to be happy, and we didn't know anything less. She prayed a lot and taught us to be thankful even when we had nothing. She would tell us every day, "Y'all girls have to be thankful for what you have."

It's amazing how I look around this big world, and see so many things people should be happy about. They have beautiful homes, fancy expensive cars, and more clothes than they'll ever wear. They have all these designer clothes like Gucci and Fendi, and they still complain. They're just not happy. They're not thankful for anything.

I got my attitude about thankfulness from my mother. She taught me to be thankful when you had nothing compared to the rest of the world. She taught us how to have integrity, and she taught us character. She taught us to say, "Yes ma'am" and "no ma'am." We learned to say "please" and "thank you." We learned to respect people.

It is sad that there is almost no respect among our kids today. The kids are being raised by families that are seeking their own identities instead of concentrating on how their kids will turn out. Of course not every family is in this shape, but there are too many in our country that are.

Kids are running the homes instead of the other way around. My mother never let us run the affairs of our home. My mother managed the house, and she forced us to mind her and pay attention. She made good people out of us. Not one of her kids ever went to jail, and that spells success in the world I grew up in. This is how my life began.

My father's name was Ersey Staton. He was born somewhere in Alabama. I never knew where my daddy was born. His mother was a white woman although some say she was Italian. Her farm was way back in the woods, and I never learned how she got that far back in the woods with that much land.

My grandmother was reputed to be very mean and unfriendly. She lived with her sister, and they were both evil according to all the people who knew them or about them. They ran a whiskey still somewhere in the woods behind their house. I have always thought of my grandmother, who I never met, as Granny on the Beverly Hillbillies only an evil Granny.

One of the most colorful stories about my Italian grandmother concerned the police. She was so mean they wouldn't go to her house. The story goes that there was a bridge in front of my mean grandmother's house. The bridge allowed people to pass the house, and she didn't like it. She would come out and yell at everybody telling them not to come across the bridge again. She would cuss them out and warn them not to cross the bridge with their wagons.

My grandmother would flash her little shotgun to show she meant what she was saying. The threats didn't stop the folks from driving over the bridge, so one day she followed through with her warnings and burned the bridge down.

My grandma's sister was even meaner than she was. Every drunk in the community would find their way to grandma's cabin to get drunk. It was said that she had the best whiskey in the State and could throw the best party in that neck of the woods. There was drinking and gambling and sometimes sex. She would have sex with her customers and as a result, she had children. My father told me one time that she had given birth to five babies as a result of her escapades.

One of the things that bothered me while growing up was why my daddy drank so much. He was weird – strange may be the better word. He was a little guy with a small frame. Part of his strangeness had to do with his lack of ability to communicate when he was sober. He barely talked. He would only talk when he was drunk.

He had mood swings all the time and when those were happening, I would just look at his face and watch him staring into space. He walked through the barns and the cotton fields by himself. He looked so sad. Looking back at how he grew up and how he was raised, he must have felt so alone, unwanted, and unloved. He lacked so much. He was never nurtured properly as a baby or as a normal child would have been.

My daddy never owned anything valuable in his life. He worked other people's land but never owned an acre of his own. The land we lived on belonged to my mother, and the title was in her name. He must never have felt like much of a man.

Whenever my mom and dad would fuss about something, she always reminded him that the property he was living on belonged to her. It was her land, her house, and her property. I am sure this contributed to whatever insecurities he possessed.

My daddy was like two different people living in the same body. He would drink with his friends every Friday and Saturday. He would sober up on Sunday and be ready for work on Monday. I blamed him for our hard life, and I didn't like him. Today, I completely understand why he was the way he was. He had pain that so many of us go through that is especially tough for a man.

Mr. Johnson was an old family friend of ours, and he was very knowledgeable about many things. He was a very well off guy at least by our standards at that time. He was a contractor that built beautiful homes, so he had the best house in our community.

Sometimes Mr. Johnson would come to our house to see me. He would tell me story after story about all the people he knew, which was just about everybody. He would say that my grandmother's sister was actually more evil than my grandmother. My grandmother would get pregnant, but she would birth all her babies.

My aunt didn't want any children, but there was no birth control back then, so she would get pregnant. She would birth the babies. Mr. Johnson said that after the babies were born, my aunt would head to the hog pen. She was seen throwing her baby to the hogs.

I can't imagine a mother being so heartless and cruel and so cold as to dispose of a child this way. I guess she isn't much different than the mothers who kill their children before they're born.

My father survived that cold, calculated home atmosphere until he was eleven years old. My daddy saw just about everything you could imagine without the help of the TV. He experienced some of the wickedest people that ever lived, and he saw it all firsthand. Can you imagine what went through the mind of a child living in those conditions, and how it would shape their character in the future?

I am glad I got to talk to Mr. Johnson because he knew more about our family than anyone else. I was sad when he passed away a few years ago.

All five of my grandmother's children were beautiful. My Uncle Joe was very handsome. You could barely tell the difference between a white guy and him. He formed a gang and got killed robbing a bank. I am not sure what happened to the rest of them, but Mr. Johnson did tell me that my Aunt Maggie and Aunt Lena were beautiful women. He said the last time he saw them they were boarding a bus and leaving town. They were never seen again in those parts. Perhaps they moved to another town and survived there.

We had a cousin, who was somehow related to that bunch. She went to school and got an education. Her name was Bessie Staton. She was a black woman with white features. Bessie told us the story about the turning point in my dad's life.

My dad was eleven years old, and he had done something really bad to make my grandmother angry. She was about to give him the worse punishment you could think of to put on a child. My grandmother told him that if he continued to be bad and misbehave, act crazy, be stupid, and kept talking too much, she would kill him.

I know my father, so it all went in one ear and out the other, so he kept being mischievous and aggravating.

Bessie used to come to our house and hang around Saturday and Sunday and tell us stories. She was a great orator. She spoke very proper and had great diction. She was a delight to listen to. She would tell us ghost stories, and we would be too scared to go to bed. We would run and scream, and it was so much fun. Cousin Bessie was amazing.

She told us this story one day about our father, who wouldn't quit being bad. My grandmother told him she was going to punish him, and so she did. She grabbed him and dragged him to a tree. Somehow she got him up the tree and tied him to a limb. She then put grass all around the tree and set it on fire.

Soon the fire was so hot and started moving up the tree. The flames finally reached my dad and set his pants on fire. He was crying and screaming for his life. My Cousin Bessie and Tom Staton were down the road in the house. They heard my father screaming, so they ran towards the burning tree. They were able to reach him in time to put out the fire and rescue him.

Tom and Bessie put my daddy in their wagon and took him home with them. The little boy was scared to death and shaking. He didn't realize his mother could be that serious as to want to burn him to death just for being a boy.

My father stayed with Tom and Bessie until he was nineteen years old. During his time growing up in Bessie's home, he was a hardworking little kid. He never learned to read and write, but he was industrious in looking for work. He could never sit still very long and always had to be occupying his time doing something. I think I inherited a lot of my energy from my father.

At eighteen or nineteen years of age, my daddy started hanging out at the juke joints. He would go there with my Uncle Walter, who was my mother's brother. My father would get half drunk and then start talking. He would talk more than anyone else and would tell funny jokes getting everybody laughing. When he was drinking, he turned into a comedian.

Somehow he found favor with my uncle. My uncle told him they had a lot of work and asked him if he would be interested in coming to work for his family. Daddy said, "yes," so he moved into my grandmother's house and lived in a back room.

Uncle Walter, Uncle Robert, Uncle Jeff, Uncle Benjamin, and Uncle Earl were all brothers living in the house. They had one sister living there, and her name was Rosie.

My daddy was a very good-looking man with curly hair and blue eyes. He had lots of energy and a great personality when he was drinking. Everybody loved my daddy when he was drinking because he became the life of the party.

Rosie was about eleven years old when my daddy came to live with her family. My father's reaction when he first saw that little girl was oh, oh, oh, what a pretty little girl.

Daddy would put her on his knee and sweet talk to her. Daddy would tell that little Rosie, "Little girl, I gonna a wait on you."

Wait on her he did and when she turned thirteen years old, my Uncle Walter allowed her to marry my dad. He took them up to the courthouse and signed the marriage license. Rosie is my mother.

My daddy was much older than she was but in those days, it didn't matter. Parents at that time were looking for a man that could provide a good living and a hard worker that would look after the children.

My mother was a beautiful woman. She was dark complexioned and had long curly hair. She was also part American Indian. She was a quiet little girl – very shy and blushed easily, and my daddy called her "babe."

My mother wasn't much of a talker unless she was with her girlfriends. I used to hear them gossiping on the back porch. My sister, Maggie, and I learned a lot about what was going on in the community by eaves dropping on the gossipy women on the back porch. Sometimes my mom would catch us and run us away, but everybody would laugh at the nosy little girls listening to the community news.

CHAPTER TWO

Mama I Love You,
and I Thought You'd Like to Know

My mother never had a child until she was nineteen years old. After Daddy and she married, for some reason, she was unable to get pregnant. At the age of nineteen, she got pregnant with their first child, and she started having kids.

I remember one time when we were about six or seven years old, we were eavesdropping on one of mother's conversations with her girlfriends. There were no doors in our rooms. In order to have some privacy, there were curtains that hung between the rooms. The curtains didn't reach all the way to the floor; so my sister and I could listen to the women talk, laugh at their jokes, and gossip.

The women didn't talk like they did around us. They would gossip about other people and then laugh about it. That particular day, my sister and I were standing very close to the curtain and taking in everything we could hear. We had no idea the ladies could see our feet. The toes of our little black shoes sticking out from under the curtain gave us away.

My mother had tipped-toed around the back of the room we were standing in and when we saw her, she had a little switch in her hand. She had sneaked right upon us, and then starting hitting on our little legs with the switch. We fled the room screaming and hollering, and I thought my mom's girlfriends would never stop laughing. Those are little funny things that happened sometimes while we were growing up.

Daddy was a hard worker. I can't count the times that I used to walk behind my father when he was plowing the grounds. I loved to feel the cold, cold earth under my bare feet. He would get up about four o'clock in the morning, and I would get up with him. I would put my little dress on with no shoes, and I'd walk behind him so happily humming and singing as he turned the earth. Every time he turned the dirt, I would walk on it, and I loved to feel the cold soft dirt under my feet, my bare feet.

Sometimes, I stayed with Daddy all day. I was the one kid that loved being with him. Wherever he went, I would follow him. We had a watermelon patch. Daddy would take me down to the watermelon patch, and we would find us a watermelon. Daddy would hit it with his fist, break it open, and we would sit there on the edge of the field, and he would talk to me about things like I was a grown up person.

Daddy would tell me stuff about my mother. He would say she don't do me right. He would say she did this and that, and then he would say,

"You know that's wrong, right?

"Yes sir, yes sir," I would answer.

 Daddy would hit the watermelon with his bare fist and open it up, and we would dig in the juicy mess with our bare hands. He'd take half of it, and I would take the other half, and my watermelon would be dripping all over my face. We would be having such a good time. Then he'd get up, and we'd start again. I would be right behind him as he walked the fields. In the wintertime when he would start working in the coalmines, I would run down the dirt road. Oh my

God, I loved running barefooted down those old dusty roads just feeling full of life. My daddy would always leave something in his lunch bucket for me. It might be nothing but an apple or a piece of bread but always a little something that he would pick up somewhere just for me. He'd give me his lunch bucket and tell me to look in there. "I got something for you." He would say.

I can see my daddy to this day walking down those dusty roads coming home from a hard day's work in the coalmines. I wish I had spent more time with my daddy, but I am thankful that I did get enough time with him to get know him and love him.

On the weekends in our house, Daddy would always have a party. I guess he learned that from his mother, but he would always bring every drunk you could think of to our home. We would have the party house of the city.

We always called our little city the Colony. The reason they called it the Colony was because at the end of slavery, they would bring the black people down there and give them a little portion of land. This is one of the most decent and admirable things that was done for the freed slaves that had no place to go or any way to make a living. They built their own little town, and everybody in the city was black. There were no white people living near the Colony. I remember the graveyard behind our Methodist Church had two Indian graves, and it is amazing how much history abounds in that little place.

The real city that we lived in was actually registered as Hanceville, Alabama. It was located in Cullman County. Segregation was a real problem back then. I was always looking at and influenced by the race relations during those times. It was horrible for us. I saw so many terrible things happening between the whites and the blacks during those days I was growing up that would have an impact on me the rest of my life.

I remember my mother taking us to town. We referred to it as town, but it was really the center of the city. Every Saturday we would run into folks who were picketing at us. They would jeer at us and say:

"Oh look, look, here come some niggers, here come the niggers, ooh wee."

They would be screaming at us and picking at us, and my mother would hold my hand. I would be so scared of them because I'd heard about the Ku Klux Klan and all of those people, and I would be scared that they were going to kill us.

There were many race related incidents that happened during those times. We never knew what was going to happen between our home and the fifteen miles we had to travel in order to buy our groceries at the general store in Hanceville. Segregation was a serious problem.

I remember many times seeing the Ku Klux Klan coming through our neighborhood blowing their horns and creating all kinds of ruckus to scare us. They carried torches because they would be after somebody in our neighborhood, and my mother would tell us to get under the bed and don't come out for any reason. We were afraid and so, so scared.

The black guy they were after was captured and either being beaten up or castrated. I hate to talk about this or tell this story because it was so gruesome, but the horror was part of our daily lives.

The Cullman County Bridge was the one you may have seen pictures of where there was a sign clearly seen by everyone passing over it, "Run Nigger Run. If You Cant Read, Run Anyway." I saw that sign every time we crossed over the Cullman County Bridge. They finally painted over the sign, so it is not there anymore.

One of the bizarre things that would happen was black men would get beaten up as a result of a spat they would have with their wives. White ladies in the community hired black women to serve in their homes. They would work as cleaning women or do the washing and ironing, and many of them worked as cooks in the white homes.

These white women became fond of the black ladies that worked so well in the homes making them comfortable. These black servants would go home and have a battle with their husbands that evening. The next morning, the black ladies would tell the white mistress about it, and the mistress would tell her husband. The next thing you know the Klan shows up at their house because they were coming to the rescue of their wife's friend and then beat the husband to a pulp to teach him a lesson that he wasn't to be messing with the house domestics they happen to be fond of.

We all knew that the lady telling the story never meant for it to go that far, but that's the way it happened. Eventually the women in our community got together and decided that they couldn't tell or share anything going on in their homes with the white women. They knew they would be putting their families in jeopardy if the gossip continued.

Mr. Thigpen was the name of the man that owned the General Store. Everything you needed was in the store. Walmart had nothing on Mr. Thigpen. Mr. Thigpen was a really rich guy.

My daddy was a talker and a manipulator. One day he went to see Mr. Thigpen.

"Mr. Thigpen," my dad said, "I want you to loan me two hundred dollars." Back in those days, two hundred dollars was a lot of money.

Mr. Thigpen said, "So I'll tell you what. If you'll sign and give me the deeds to your property, I'll give you the two hundred dollars."

Daddy signed by putting his X on the note, and Mr. Thigpen gave my father two hundred dollars. Daddy came back to the house with a lot of stuff that he bought from Mr. Thigpen with the money. What he didn't spend on stuff, he drank the rest of it up, and gambled it away.

One Saturday morning, Mr. Thigpen shows up at our house because daddy never paid the money back. Mr. Thigpen said to my mom,

"Rosie, we came to tell you all you got to move."

"What? Move where?" My mother answered in dismay.

"We own your land now." He explained. "Ersey borrowed some money from me, and here's the contract right here where he signed his name."

My mother didn't say a word. She left the front porch and retrieved the shoebox where she kept her deeds. She gladly showed the deeds to Mr. Thigpen. My daddy's name was nowhere on them.

"Ersey is the first black dude ever beat me." Mr. Thigpen admitted. "He forever outsmarted me."

We laughed about it, but Daddy had to run for a while. He had to make himself scarce because they were after him. He looked so much like the white people that he blended in with the crowd and never got caught.

Daddy did it again to another man down the street. He sold all our pigs to the man. The man came to our house on a Saturday to pick up his pigs. My mother met him at the door.

"Ersey, don't own no pigs," my mother yelled. "These are my pigs," so they had to leave. Daddy was such a trickster. He was just different. He got away with so, so much.

My daddy would make friends with everybody and invite them all to the parties he threw at our house. Mr. Thigpen came a couple of times after he got over losing the two hundred dollars my daddy skinned out of him. People liked him for some reason. Everybody liked him. He had a lot of favor with white guys and their families. Mexican families loved him as did his own black people. Daddy was the person; he was like an entertainer. People followed him around, and he'd bring them all to the house.

Daddy was a fisherman, too. He loved to fish. He would go out on Friday and Saturday evenings and sometimes during the weekdays when he got off work and had some time on his hands. He and his friends would go fishing, so we'd have a lot of fish. We didn't have a refrigerator because they didn't have them back then, so the iceman would come by, and we would buy fifty pounds of ice and fill up the icebox. Mama would fish fry on Saturday. We would have a fish fry at our house with our friends, and daddy would bring out the RCA Victrola.

The Victrola was a large device that played records. There was no electricity back where we lived, so the Victrola was kept going by turning a crank on the side of the cabinet. They gave me the job of turning the handle, and my little hand would be so tired keeping the music going. I would complain about being so tired, but daddy would say, "Keep that music going."

The folks would be out there in the middle of our front room dancing around the potbellied stove. There were people dancing everywhere. They would be dancing and drinking from the front yard through the house to the back yard. They all talked at once and were very loud. It was just amazing. We had a party, party, party house.

My mother would go along with it for a while, and then she'd get sick of everybody and run them off. I can't count the times when my two older sisters had to fight drunken men, who were trying to seduce them sexually. Somehow, they always fought them off. We were so blessed to be virgins until we were in our late teens. We could've been raped and even murdered, but God kept his hand over us because every kind of man you could think of would be over at our little house. It didn't matter to some whether they were black or white. I remember my mother was always in the kitchen frying chicken and fish for them. We raised our own chickens, so all they had to do was go outside and get a chicken and kill it, cut it up, and fry it.

Daddy also had a still and made his own whiskey. The still was behind the house way back in the woods. One day, somebody turned him in. My mother told me that when my brother Sam was about a year old, my father was arrested for making whiskey. He went to jail for a year and a day. He was convicted twice for the same thing. My daddy quit making whiskey when my sister, Katherine, was born and then passed away. My mother said something turned inside of him that made him stop taking those chances.

CHAPTER THREE

You Can Make It

Daddy was fine during the week but when the weekends came around, he was just like the O'Jays song *Living for the Weekend.* It was party time at the Staton house. It didn't matter, he'd go out and invite everybody, and the place would be full of bodies.

Men would congregate on the front porch and start fussing at each other, and they would be discussing the conditions of the world. Nobody had any facts, so they would just talk total nonsense. This went on until my mother got tired of them, and she would tell them,

"Why don't you all people get out of here, go, and get out of here!"

The strange thing was they wouldn't mess around with her. They would get up and go. Daddy would pile so many of them in an old truck, and they would leave the property.

I wanted to sing. I really wanted to sing, and that is about all

I ever wanted to do. My singing career began as a little girl. My mother would take me to church every Sunday even when she was carrying me. When the church doors were open, I was there.

As a baby, I loved to hear the people sing and listen to the music. I loved singing and music when I didn't even know what they were all about. When you are brought up in a certain environment and are around something all your life, it becomes a normal part of you. All the knowledge we had whether it be politics or music, we learned at our local church.

No one in our family or in the community was fantastic out front singers. We had average church choirs, but we loved to sing. I loved my sisters Maggie and Lillie, but Maggie was my favorite. Both of us wanted to sing, so we learned all the songs we could both religious and popular music. We listened to the songs until we knew them by heart.

We had this old radio that looked like a car battery. The reception was terrible, and the static was annoying, but we would listen to all the stations on the air whether it was Rhythm and Blues, country music, or gospel. We listened to them all. There were only three AM stations, but they played all kinds of music.

Country living was boring, so we made our time entertaining ourselves by learning how to harmonize, and our goal was to become the best singers in the neighborhood.

We had two churches in our community. On the first and third Sundays, we would go to the Methodist church. On the second and fourth Sundays, we would attend the Baptist church. Every fifth Sunday the churches would get together and have a singing convention.

People would come from everywhere. Folks would travel from Sipsey, Jasper, Warrior, and the big city of Birmingham. Every town around had somebody on the church grounds for that convention. The place was packed with people. The churches would bring their choirs, chorales, duets and solo singers, and there would be an all day singing with dinner on the grounds.

People would bring food and share it. We would put little pallets on the ground or blankets, and the food would be put out, so everybody could come around with their plates and have some food. Everyone knew to bring their own plates because there was no paper plates back then, so you either brought your own plate or stopped at the store on the way in and purchased a tin plate to eat on.

Black eyed peas, potato salad, greens, fried chicken, roast beef, fried fish, and then it all got topped off with some of the most delicious desserts this side of heaven. Those ladies would make every kind of pie imaginable, and there is nothing like homemade pies. You can't beat homemade chocolate cake. The coconut cakes and homemade sweet potato pies were to die for. Custards of every flavor imaginable could be found on those blankets full of food.

We loved Nehi drinks. You could buy orange and grape sodas, but my favorite was always strawberry Nehi. It was amazing how people would be at these events. The kids jumped rope and played ball during the break. We'd sing for two or three hours, and then everybody would head out for the dinner. We would eat and play and then head back to the church for more hours of singing. I couldn't wait for the fifth Sunday to roll around.

One of those Sundays really sticks out in my mind and has stayed with me all these years. I was only four years old when it happened, and I will never forget it.

A family showed up with this little girl. She was maybe seven years old but man could she sing. They put her up on the platform, and she began to sing. Oh my, her voice reverberated throughout the entire church, and she wasn't using a microphone.

I sat there completely aware that this might be the greatest voice I ever heard. My sister and I were both in awe of this child. We sat there listening, and our eyes were wide open as we stared her down.

On the way home, we told each other that if that little girl could sing that good, then so could we.

When we were home, we started singing. We tried to sing, but we couldn't. We were so shook up and shaky that nothing would come out right, and so we prayed.

My sister and I had what we called our "praying tree." About a minute up the road from our house was a tree that had blown over. We'd go up there and get on our knees and start calling out to the

Lord. We would pray, "Lord, let us sing. We want to sing like that little girl."

We never could sing like that girl. We would go back up to the church, and we would join with some of the chorales that churches would bring to the singings. They used to teach music by do-re-me- fa- so- la- ti- do. This was a sequence of notes on the scale that people used to practice staying on key.

One of my favorite songs that I loved to sing using this method was do-re-mi-fa-fa-do-re-mi. I would sing it like this: do-re-do-re-do-re-mi, fa-fa-do-re-mi, oh do-re-dum-dum-dum-de-dum-dum, and the crowd would start singing, "Some glad morning when this life is o're, I'll fly away."

Everybody would be clapping in time with the music, and you could hear his or her feet tapping on the wooden floor. Maggie and I were determined that we had to learn how to sing.

In the summertime about six or seven months after the big singing convention was over, people from this church came up from Birmingham. They went to the Baptist church and said they wanted to come up and have a revival. They were told by some of the folks that they would have to go see the pastor about it.

They did see the pastor, and he told them, "no," so they went over to the Methodist church and sought out the pastor and asked him the same question. Could they run a revival? The Methodist pastor told them the same thing.

"We don't want no revivals being run up here," the pastor told them.

Not being deterred, the Birmingham group starting going house to house asking people if they could use their homes to begin a revival meeting. Every house they went to told them the same thing.

"We don't have no room. We don't want no revival up here."

These Holiness people came to our house. I saw the old car they were driving pull up. They got out of the car and told my mother that they were looking for a place where they could praise God.

"We want to run a revival," the leader said. "We don't care where it is as long as we can use your property. You don't have to do anything, ma'am; just let us do it here. Can we use your yard?"

My mother looked at the men and said, "Of course you can."

The day the meeting started, a few people showed up in a small bus. There were maybe seven or eight of them. They brought out some little drums and some tambourines. They sat down and started singing, "Take the Lord along witch ya, everywhere ya go."

They had a drumbeat like nobody's business. My sister and I had never heard anything like that in our entire lives. They were slinging and beating those drums, and we were buck dancing the whole time. We bucked danced right in front of them, and they loved every minute of it.

Mama was sitting on the porch watching us and smiling from ear to ear. She was getting a kick out of watching us dance. My little brother Robert started buck dancing with us. He was amazing. We'd never see the little guy dance like that.

It wasn't long before a few people driving by would stop by the road. They got out of their cars and stood behind the bus watching it all happen. They wouldn't dare come closer because someone said that those people talk some kind of funny language called speaking in tongues. They would throw some magic dust on you, and you'd be crazy the rest of your life.

I am so glad they threw that magic dust on me, and I got crazy, and you know what, I'm still crazy today. That old magic dust worked, and we got blessed. My mother got blessed.

After the revival was over, Maggie and I kept the beat going. We got a bucket and two big sticks. One of us beat the bucket while the other buck danced. We sang the same songs, and we made the same beat. We loved this new religion.

One day, Maggie and I looked at each other. We realized something we never knew before. We could sing. Our voices were changing, and we could sing. I was thinking, *Oh my God, I am five years old, and I can sing!*

God handed down our gifts to us. In our house, there was no way we could learn music. There was nothing available for us to learn by. I believe it was by my mother's obedience that we received our gifts and from that day forward, we started singing.

Since my sister was the bold one, she took the first steps. We would listen to the radio stations, and then she would sing. We listened to the gospel stations and learned how to sing runs. We idolized Mahalia Jackson, and we studied The Mighty Clouds of Joy. We listened to Edna Gallmon Cooke and the Five Blind Boys. We heard and studied all the great Gospel singers.

We turned to the blues stations. We loved B.B. King and Bobby "Blue" Bland. We learned our runs from songs like *Mama He Treats Your Daughter Mean*. "He's the meanest man I've ever seen." We learned our runs from those old classic blues songs.

We listened to the Country Music stations. We loved Ernest Tubb and starting listening to all the great country singers of that time. One of our favorite songs was *I'm sending you a big bouquet of roses, one for every time you broke my heart*.

We came up with a style all our own. Gospel, Gospel/Blues and Country. We kept singing, and we kept growing up. When I was about five and a half years old, my sister had to go to school. I was in the back of the house singing and making mud pies when Miss Ella Cannon, my mother's girlfriend, came to the house. As she was walking up the hill, she heard me singing.

Miss Ella stopped to listen. This was no ordinary voice coming from this little five and a half year old girl. Miss Ella came in to the house and found my mother.

"Rosie, did you know your little girl can sing?" She said.

"Ah, I hear that all the time," my mother replied.

"Rosie, she can sing," Miss Ella said. "This girl has talent."

Miss Ella Cannon went to our Pastor, Reverend King, and told him that he had an amazing talent in his church. She told him about me.

The next Sunday, the Pastor surprised everybody and especially me. He called me to the platform to sing. I was shaking all over. I had never sung before an audience – I had never performed before anybody except Maggie and my mom.

I started walking up the aisle toward the podium and thinking *What am I going to do?* I was scared, and then I thought about that little girl, who sang so beautifully in our church. I thought that I would go up there and sing just as beautifully as she did. *She wasn't scared, so I ain't scared either.*

When I walked up the stairs to the platform, there were bannisters with a curtain that encircled the stage. I was too small to look over the top, so people could see me, so they stood me on a chair. I looked at the crowd and bravely started singing *The Lord Will Make a Way Somehow*. "When beneath the cross I bow, He will take away your burdens. Let Him have your burdens now. When the load gets heavy, and the weight is showing up on your brow, there's a sweet relief in knowing, oh the Lord will make a way somehow."

The entire church was standing on their feet clapping and singing. I jumped off the chair and immediately ran to my mom. That started it all. Maggie and I started singing duets, and we sang almost every Sunday for the church and Reverend King.

Pastor King would get invited to preach in other churches. Almost every time he made a trip, he would ask my mother if we could go with him. She gladly let us go, and the preacher started drawing some big crowds that were coming to hear the two little singing girls.

When I started to school, every day Maggie and I would sing. The other kids wanted us to sing for them, so we happily complied. It was our passion. Soon, some other girls got interested in singing. Betty Jean Byers and Letha Mae Malcolm could sing. We began harmonizing during our recesses and lunch breaks.

Letha Mae's Aunt Elizabeth was our church pianist. She started practicing with us and helped us form a group. We called ourselves the Four Golden Echoes. We traveled all over Alabama singing in churches everywhere, and people would come from all over and fill up those churches to hear us sing.

We were around Southern white folks the most, so we picked up that southern drawl. We didn't talk like normal people. We used to sing a song I'm Climbing High Mountains Trying to Get Home.

We would sing, "I'm clamming high mountains. I'm clamming high mountains trying to git home. I'm clamming, clamming, clamming…"

There was a schoolteacher listening to us one day. After we were through "clamming," she came up to us and said, "I want to talk to you little girls. You don't say clamming, you say climbing. Now let me hear you say climbing."

"Climbing, climbing, climbing, I'm climbing," I said distinctly.

"Now that's what you say," She said. "Don't ever let me hear you say 'clamming' again okay?"

We said, "Yes ma'am. Thank you ma'am."

We started that day watching our enunciation of words. It was so much fun traveling and singing. After we were through performing, we would get invited over to a pastor's house or someone in the church and have the most wonderful food. We were treated like famous singers, and I guess in our own little way, the Four Golden Echoes were famous.

CHAPTER FOUR

Grace, That's Why They Call It Amazing

Everybody thought my daddy was a heathen. He had no religion, didn't go to church, and he didn't care what people said about him. He cursed a lot and cussed all the time. Still, he was so proud of us as we were singing and going from church to church all over the State.

I learned to curse from my daddy. As a little girl, I could curse with the best of them. I was just like my daddy. My mama would remind me every day just how much like my daddy I was.

"You just like your old daddy," she would say.

My daddy got me drunk when I was ten years old. He mixed some sugar and water together and poured some whiskey in it. People called it a hot toddy. It was given to you when you were a little sick or had the flu. It tasted like a tea. I drank the hot toddy, and daddy and I were sitting on the front porch both of us drunk.

I got up and stumbled all around. I was trying to find a place to pee, and daddy was laughing his fool head off. Mama kept telling him to stop taking me with him to the joints. It was ruining me, and then he would take me gambling with him. I started growing and getting bigger, daddy would have me while he was gambling with six or seven men. I would be sitting there in my little dress. We didn't wear pants in those days, so daddy would rub the dice on my leg, "7 come 11," and throw them. When 7 or 11 came up, the men would put their money in my lap.

My daddy said I was his good luck charm because every time I went with him, and he rubbed my leg, he'd win. We kept what we were doing from my mother for a long time. She was taking me to church on Sunday, and daddy was taking me to hell on Saturday.

Daddy kept all his money in my dress. I'd be sitting there with all this money and cursing with the men. I could curse. I knew every curse word in the vocabulary of the curse word dictionary. There was nothing I wouldn't say, and I hung with my daddy all the time. I had the best of both worlds.

I was a drunk and a gambler at ten years old, and I was the soloist at church on Sunday. I was also a thief. Mama made little pockets in my dresses. When my lap was full of money, I would take some when nobody was looking and hide it in my pockets. I did this for mama. I would take the money home and let mama find it, so she could have some money to buy some things for herself.

"Now don't you tell your mama I brought you out here," my daddy would say every time we finished our gambling. "You better never say nothing about this. It's our secret."

"No, sir," I would reply. "I ain't telling a living soul nothing about this."

The weekends were so fun for me, and things would be back to normal on Monday with mama telling me I was just like my daddy.

"Yeah, right." I would say.

Daddy loved to hear us sing. He would hear us sometimes singing at parties. When we were home and daddy was throwing one of his parties, he'd take off his old hat he wore.

"You girls come on over here and sing for your daddy," he would say.

Maggie and I would start off singing, and those old drunks at the party would start crying and saying, "Jesus, help me Lord, help me Jesus. Y'all sing so good oh Lord I need to change. Lord I need to change my ways. Lord have mercy."

Those drunken men didn't know anything about anointing, but I knew that God had his hand on me. He had His hand on me my entire life.

I have already told about how slick my daddy was. At seven, eight, nine years old, we were singing for the drunks at our house. Mama would get on daddy about his drinking. She'd say,

'Ersey, you better stop your drinking and teaching these girls how to cuss. You're going to hell if you don't stop this."

"I ain't going to hell," he'd tell her. "These girls are going to sing me to heaven."

After we would be done singing for the drunks, daddy would take off his old hat and start passing it around. He was taking up an offering.

"Now pay em, pay up, every one of y'all pay them girls." Daddy would tell the drunks as he passed the hat. Crooked Ersey Staton.

They would put in two or three dollars. Daddy never gave any of the money to us. He'd keep it for himself and then go buy some whiskey. Oh my God, it is amazing how I grew up.

My oldest brother was Sam, and he quit going to school when he was in the ninth grade. He dropped out of school to help work. He worked the fields for other people and did it to help my mother raise us. He was a surrogate father to us.

Sam really was like a dad to us. He was more a dad than he was an older brother. He always looked after us because daddy was the playboy and was never around much. Sam was a serious boy. He went to work early every day. He helped load trucks picking up beans and other crops, and then he would head to the cotton fields and pick cotton till late evening and then come home. He was only fourteen or fifteen years old when he was working this hard for the family.

Sam wouldn't spend his money on himself. Every weekend, he would bring all the money he made home. He would give the money to mama, so she could buy food and things for us that we needed. He made sure we had something.

Some of our cousins had moved to Cleveland, Ohio. They told Sam he ought to come up there and get a job like they had. They had told him when they left that they would get jobs and a nice place to live and then send for him to come and find work.

They did send for Sam. They had jobs and nice places to live, and they told Sam he could make a lot more money than he could down in Alabama, and he could also send money home to mama and the girls.

Sam left home when he turned eighteen years old, and I hated to see him leave. It was like he had died. Sam stabilized the home, and he was the one we looked up to for guidance and security. He was strong.

Daddy was weak, and he got beat up a lot. He would run his mouth and get a fight started, and then he would end up getting beat up. Sam never wanted to be like daddy.

It was a sad day when Sam left for Cleveland. We got in our cars and rode with him to the bus station. Mama was crying, Maggie and I were crying. We didn't want to let him go.

"Daddy stop him," I cried. "Mom stop him. Don't let him go. Sam, please don't go."

"I got to do this," Sam replied. "I can't live like this and mama, y'all can't live like this no more, either. When I get up to Cleveland, I'm going to get a house and when I've earned enough money, I'm going to get y'all a house and bring you up there."

Sam wrote to us when he got to Cleveland. We didn't have a phone, so the only way to communicate was by mail. In one of his letters, Sam told us he met a lady. *Her name is Ethel,* he wrote. *I think I'm going to get married.*

Sam and Ethel got married, and they found themselves a house. They moved out to Twinsburg, Ohio about thirty or forty miles outside of Cleveland. It was in the country but compared to where we lived in the country, it was really upscale. They didn't have a well with a pump. They had water running through the house. They called it "running water," and that was different to hear about.

About eighteen months after Sam moved to the Cleveland area, he wrote to mama and told her to get us ready to move because he had a place for us to live. He told mama that daddy was never going to change so get on out of there.

I will never forget the day when mama told us we were moving to Cleveland. She told us not to tell daddy, so we waited one morning for him to go to work. Mama packed up everything we had. We didn't have suitcases, so she had gone to Mr. Thigpen's store and got some boxes for us. She put our names on our personal box, and we put in our clothes and some of our favorite little things we owned.

One of mama's girlfriends heard that we were moving to Cleveland, so she told everybody in the community to keep it a secret from our daddy. One of their little kids had grown out of a snowsuit, and they decided that it would fit Canzetta. They also said we would need it in Cleveland worse than somebody would down in Alabama, so they gave the snowsuit to me instead of giving it to another kid living in the area.

We were ready to go. Instead of waiting until we got to Cleveland, mama put the snowsuit on me. It was October in Alabama and still very warm. Sam had gotten my brother, Joe, out of Alabama and up to Cleveland. He then got my oldest sister up there, so everybody was gone except mama, Maggie, Robert, and me. We had to find a neighbor to drive us to the bus station.

My mother had put the snowsuit on me, and everybody was looking at her like she'd lost her mind.

"You better keep that snowsuit on, girl, because it's gonna be cold where we're going up in Cleveland." My mama said.

"But it's not cold now," I complained. "Please let me take it off. It's too hot."

"Keep it on," she said. "Because you're going to need it."

"Lord have mercy," I whispered

We got on the Greyhound Bus, and people were snickering and giggling.

"Little girl, ain't that snowsuit a little hot for this time of year?" They laughed.

"Not really," I replied.

They looked at us like the true Beverly Hillbillies. We looked crazy.

We went to the back of the bus because at that time black folks couldn't sit up front on busses. We were sitting in the back as the bus began the journey, and it got hotter and hotter in the snowsuit. I took part of it off and rolled it down around my waist, and I started fanning to stay cool. However, the closer we got to Cleveland, the cooler the weather became.

We stopped at rest stops, and I would have to roll the snowsuit back up in order to stay warm. We arrived in Cleveland, and mama was absolutely right. We stepped off the bus and into snow.

There was snow everywhere, and it was snowing. I had no cap on my head, so I pulled the snowsuit up over my head, and I was smiling at everybody. I was looking at them and thinking *All right. All right. Y'all ain't ready for this weather. Go ahead and pick at me why don't you.*

When we got off the bus, my brother was there to meet us, and his wife Ethel was with him. We met her for the first time, and she was so nice. She smiled at us and said,

"I am so glad to see you all. Welcome to Cleveland."

We piled into Sam's car and crammed in our boxes. Sam, Ethel, mama, Maggie, Robert, and I were all squished into the car riding out of Cleveland to where Sam and Ethel lived.

We kept driving and driving and when mama asked how far, Sam reminded us that they lived a ways from Cleveland in a little town named Twinsburg. The closer we got to Twinsburg, the more country the surroundings became. I thought, *this is country.*

"We're home." Sam said.

The house had an old pot bellied stove in the front room and there were two bedrooms. There was a kitchen and another little room in the back we would call the "backroom." It was probably made for a sewing room, but it had just enough room for a rollaway bed.

Ethel had really done a lot of work fixing the place, so we'd be comfortable and feel at home. Ethel told us where we would each be sleeping, and Maggie and I would sleep together. Maggie was thirteen, and I was eleven, and we had to sleep in this tiny bed. Sam and Ethel had two kids, so they slept in the same room with their parents. It all worked out.

Sam's kids would sometimes sleep in our room in their tiny bed, but they started loving us, and we loved them back. Lillie was there. She had moved in with them, so the house was full of people.

They had an old fashioned Maytag washing machine. We washed a lot of clothes and had to hang them on the lines outside. I was thinking, *this ain't much different than the place we left in Alabama.* It was cold up there.

Our honeymoon was broken quickly because we had to enroll in school the first Monday we were there. We were going to have to wait for our transcripts coming from Alabama, and it would take a long time because everything was transported through the mail.

They surmised which class we should be in, so they put us in a classroom that I knew there was no way I should be there. The lessons started coming, and I started sweating. They were so far ahead of us that it was like sitting in a foreign language class in another country. When they started throwing math, English, history, and all the other subjects at us, I was in a fog. I looked like the country fool dummy sitting with those kids. The teacher would call me to the board and ask me to solve a math problem, and I had never seen any arithmetic like that in my whole life. I was a nervous wreck. I couldn't sleep at night, and I didn't know what to do.

Before we went to this new school, we had a lot to learn. We were very backward country girls. One of the funny things that happened concerned a store that was on the corner near the house.

Sam told us one day to go to the store and get some potatoes. Sam said get some white potatoes, and tell the storekeeper to put them in a bag. Maggie and I skipped on up to the store and walked in.

"You must be Sam's sisters," the storekeeper said. Sam had already called up there and told him we were coming. "What do you girls want?"

"We want some white taters and a poke to put 'em in." We explained.

"What?" He asked incredulously.

"We want some white taters and a poke to put 'em in," we repeated.

"I ain't never…" the storekeeper paused.

He then called Sam on the phone. "Man what are these kids talking about?" He said. "They want something in a poke."

Sam started laughing so loud I could hear him on the phone. We got the taters in a poke and ran back home.

"You don't say taters and poke to put em in up here." Sam explained. "You say: We want some potatoes."

I said, "potaters."

"POTATOES!" Sam yelled.

"Okay, we'll say potatoes," I replied.

A funny thing happened the first night we spent in the house. We had never seen electric lights before. In the houses in Alabama where we lived, we used kerosene lamps to light the house. They hadn't wired our community with electricity yet, so we lived with kerosene lamps.

Maggie and I were so used to blowing out the flames in the lamp chimneys. They started turning off the lights in the house and told us to put out the light in our room because Sam had to get up early and go to work in the steel mill.

In our room there was a light bulb hanging from the ceiling with a chain on it that you pull to turn off the light. Maggie pulled up a chair and was stretching and blowing on the light. She blew and blew, but nothing happened. I asked her if she wanted me to help, but she insisted that she could get it out.

"What are you girls doing?" Ethel asked as she had heard the commotion and came to our room.

"I can't blow this light out." Maggie explained.

Ethel almost fell down laughing. She screamed, she laughed, and she got Sam out of bed.

"You got to see this, Sam." Ethel yelled.

Sam came in the room, and Ethel told Maggie to blow out the light. Maggie started blowing, and Sam began laughing so hard he could barely stand up.

"See that string there, Maggie? Pull on it." Sam explained.

Maggie pulled on the string, and the light went out. He told her to pull it again, and she did. The light came on.

"Now y'all go to bed." Sam instructed.

We had to go to the bathroom, so we were going outside to find the outhouse like we used down in Alabama.

"Where you all going?" Ethel asked as she saw us heading toward the door.

"We're going to the toilet," we said together.

"Come here and let me show you where the toilet is." Ethel said. "When your are finished using the toilet, flush it."

"Flush it? I asked.

"Yes. See that little string on the side of the toilet? Pull it, and the toilet will flush itself."

"I'm scared." I said nervously.

"Me too," Maggie replied.

I pulled the string, and the toilet sounded like a monster. We both ran as fast as we could and jumped into bed. We were absolutely ignorant of these things and had to learn how to function on our own in this strange society. This is the metamorphosis of changing from country life to city life. It was amazing, and we learned so much in a short amount of time. Nevertheless, I was making F's Ethel was working overtime trying to help me catch up, but it was to no avail. The teacher thought I was retarded. The kids at school were laughing and making fun of us. We felt so stupid, but we got through it.

My mother got on welfare. One night, Ethel told us that Sam said we could sing. I nodded in agreement with this observation.

"Why don't you sing me a song?" Ethel asked.

We sang a song. We sang the song to the point that Ethel was in tears.

"Sam didn't tell me you could sing like that." She said sobbing.

We sang and sang and sang that night. Song after song we sang.

"Oh, we're gonna be rich," Ethel said.

"These girls didn't come up here to get rich." My brother explained. "They came up here to better their lives, so don't be talking about somebody getting rich."

"Well, I'll tell you what," Ethel replied. "I'm going to take y'all and buy y'all some new clothes, and then I'm taking y'all to Bishop Jewell. I'm taking y'all to my church."

We went shopping. Now we didn't go to the fancy stores. We went to the thrift shops, and Ethel bought us some nice things, and she took them home and washed them. She ironed them and made us look presentable.

On that Tuesday night, they had a singing contest at the church. This church is like no church you've ever seen in your life. It was a lot like the Holiness Church in the Colony, but much more upscale with their music and instruments. They had a whole band playing for the services. They were jamming with the drums, piano, bass fiddle, guitars, and gospel steel guitar.

They were dancing, and I mean real dancing. They were jumping like they do in the clubs. They were sweating profusely, and I'm thinking, *Good Lord, what kind of church is this?*

Ethel dressed us to the nines and told us she was going to get us into the contest that night. Ethel was an outgoing person, so she told one of the ushers that she had some little girls with her that they need to let sing. We sat and waited, and I thought I was in a nightclub because of the way they were jamming and dancing to the music. I loved it, though. I couldn't do anything in school but when I got into that kind of atmosphere, I came alive.

Eventually, they called us up to the platform. Maggie and me were about to hit the big time. We knew our song backwards and forwards and up and down. The problem was we had never sung with a microphone before, and they handed one to each of us. We started singing. I can't remember what song it was because we knew so many, but we got used to the sound real quickly and started singing our hearts out.

To our surprise, the band broke in and started playing behind us. They picked up our key and were following us perfectly. We were doing something we'd never done before, and we were singing to the Glory of God. There was an atmosphere change. The place caught on fire. Everybody jumped out of his or her seats. It was a bad song. I know it was a bad song because the people were really dancing.

We started singing and jumping. We were part of the Four Gospel Echoes, and we knew how to work a crowd. That crowd was going totally wild over what we were doing up there.

Afterwards, Bishop Jewell called Ethel up to the platform and whispered something in her ear. Ethel came down towards us, and she was smiling ear to ear. Bishop Jewell was the overseer of more than thirty churches. These churches were all over the nation but mainly in Ohio, Kentucky, Tennessee, Alabama, Michigan, New York, Mississippi, and California. She owned a school named Jewell Academy and Seminary. The school taught grades one through twelve, and you were automatically accepted into Tennessee State University when you graduated from the Jewell Academy.

There were kids whose families couldn't afford the tuition but if they could sing…

CHAPTER FIVE

Love Lifted Me

The kids who belonged to Bishop Jewell's church and couldn't afford to be sent to the private schools had their tuition provided by Bishop Jewell.

After we sang at Bishop Jewell's church and she called Ethel up to talk to her, Ethel came back and told us that the Bishop wanted to talk to us. Bishop Jewell came down, and I don't believe I've ever seen a woman that big. She was at least six foot three, and she must have weighed near three hundred pounds or more. She was huge.

Bishop Jewell had a granddaughter, who was Nettie Mae Harrison. Her father was Bishop Lorenzo Harrison. They had a daughter named Naomi. Naomi was nine years old and held the distinction of being a child preacher.

Ethel came down and told us to wait for Bishop Jewell. When the big preacher left her monstrous chair she sat in on the platform, she asked us to follow her to her office.

We walked through a hallway across from the church auditorium. The office was actually in her parsonage located on Kinsman Avenue. Bishop Jewell wanted to talk to Ethel and my mother about sending us down to Nashville to the school. She told my mom the girls can sing, so they won't have to pay tuition. We would not only sing for our tuition, room and board, but we would also sing for those kids, who were there but couldn't afford tuition and also couldn't sing.

This all made me very happy because I hated the school in Twinsburg. It was driving me nuts. Bishop Jewell would stay in one place for about six weeks, and then she would move on to the next revival she was running. She had houses in all the places she had churches, and she owned parsonages where she would live. She had a fleet of beautiful fancy cars like I've never seen in my life. I couldn't believe any black people could live in that kind of luxury.

After we were introduced to Bishop Jewell, my mother went on welfare, and we moved into Cleveland. One of Ethel's family members had a home with a finished basement, so we rented the place and moved in. Mother was getting this little check every month, and we were provided food stamps. We had plenty to eat and were doing pretty good. Thank God we were out of Sam and Ethel's house in Twinsburg.

We enrolled in the Kinsman Elementary School in Cleveland. It was worse than the school in Twinsburg. At the Kinsman School, I learned about bullying. I was bullied everyday at school.

We got our transcripts from the school in Twinsburg. I thought it was hard in Twinsburg; it was a horrified nightmare at Kinsman. Those kids in the school were gangsters. I sat in front of a girl, who didn't like my long hair, so she was constantly pulling it. She was constantly challenging me to a fight.

If that weren't enough dealing with the hair-pulling girl, there was a little boy who had a girlfriend names Esther. Esther was jealous of me and was always telling me she was going to beat me up. She would tell me this every day, and she was huge. She was double jointed and had the build of a boxer. She hardly had any hair on her head and was horrible mean looking. I have to admit that I was very afraid of that chick.

Her boyfriend's name was Cleveland, and he was in the same classroom that we were in. One day, the girl came up to me and said,

"You like Cleveland, don't you?"

I am so naive. I said, "Yeah. I like Cleveland."

"I knew it," she said. "I knew it. I knew you like Cleveland. I ask you if you like Cleveland, and you said, yes I like Cleveland."

I looked at her angry face. She looked like a bull ready to charge. "I do like Cleveland, but what Cleveland are you talking about?" I nervously asked her.

" My boy friend, Cleveland." She yelled.

"No, no," I said. "I don't like your boyfriend. I don't even know him."

"Yes you do. Yes you do like him," she yelled.

"I am going to beat you. I'm going to beat you so bad you're going to wish you'd never seen Cleveland," she said as she was pushing me backwards very hard.

I took off running. I was running for my life down the hallway. Maggie was hanging around in the hall. I was dropping books, and everything else I was carrying. I yelled at Maggie to help me, and she told me,

"You got this. You're going to have to do this on your own. Run girl, you gotta learn to run."

I made it to the street, and I ran all the way down Kinsman Avenue. I was tired. Books and papers were everywhere behind me. It was horrible. I was praying to the Lord to get me out of there.

When Bishop Jewell asked my mom to let us go to Nashville, my mom told her "no." She told the Bishop that we were too young to leave home. We kept begging and begging her. We told her we can't learn in the Cleveland schools, and we were being threatened every day.

Mom was standing on the porch when Esther ran me all the way down the street.

"You better get back up there and find those books and your papers." She said. "I don't have no more money to buy you books and papers."

I was so scared. I crept back up the street toward the school hoping I wouldn't run into Esther. I stooped while picking up the books and papers and keeping one eye out for Esther. Esther was nowhere around, and I headed back to the house.

CHAPTER SIX

Music Speaks Louder Than Words

We had been living in Cleveland a little while, and I couldn't get anything going in school, and I couldn't take the abuse. Bishop Jewell was still in Cleveland, and Ethel would come by the house every Sunday to put the pressure on my mother to allow us to go to Nashville.

Sometimes all of us would have Sunday dinner together, and mama would tell Ethel that the girls were too young to go off by themselves; even though, they all knew that Bishop Jewell would treat us well.

When I begged mama to let us go, she would tell me to shut up and quit bothering her about it. We were there about four weeks after Bishop Jewell asked us to come to Nashville. We had stopped asking mama if we could go down there because we knew the deal was done. When mama said "no," that's what she meant, and there was no use bugging her anymore. Three weeks later, Bishop Jewell was about to leave for Nashville.

Daddy showed up at the door. He took a bus to Cleveland and found out where we lived and was knocking on the door. Mama eyes were as big as two moons when she opened the door, and there stood my daddy.

"What in the world are you doing here?" She asked.

"Well, I'm coming to see my children," he replied. "I'm coming to see my children, and I ain't coming up here to see you. I just want to see my children."

Mama let him in. Daddy was behaving, and they both were very quiet. They weren't saying much, but they did talk. I could hear them talking at night. We were in bed, but I could hear them discussing my daddy's demeanor.

"You haven't changed a bit," she said. "I don't know why you wanted to come up here. We've been doing just fine without you around. Now you come up here to mess everything up for us."

"I'm going to get a job," Daddy said. "I'm going to do better. Rosie, I love you, and I want us to be a family again. I promise I'm going to do better."

Daddy did pretty good for a couple of weeks. He went out every day looking for a job and finally got one. Daddy loved to work, so he got his job working for a Chinese laundry. He sort of looked like he could have some Chinese in him, so I suppose that helped him get the work. He went to work everyday, but he had to wait two weeks before he got paid.

Bishop Jewell was still in Cleveland, and about a week before she was packed and leaving for Nashville, daddy came in drunk. He was cursing and cutting up. He had spent all his money, and mama was crying.

"I knew this was going to happen," she cried. " I knew you weren't going to stay straight and act right. I told you Ersey not to come up here. Why don't you just leave us alone, and let us make something out of ourselves? Why you going to do this? Why did you come up here and ruin everything for me? Now, I got to get off welfare because you're here. You know the authorities are going to come around this house to find out who's living here, and my kids ain't going to have no food or anything else because you're here. You ain't going to do right."

A couple of nights went by, and mother walked into my bedroom. We were in bed, so she shut the door and pulled up a chair.

"You know what," she began. "I've decided I'm going to let y'all go with that lady. I'm going to let y'all go with that woman, and maybe she can do more for y'all than I can. "

We jumped out of bed and started jumping up and down and hugging each other. We hugged mama.

"You won't regret this mama. We're going to make you proud," we yelled. "We'll take care of you. We'll help take care of you."

Bishop Jewell came to see us after she found out we could go down to Nashville. She talked to mama.

"You won't have to worry about a thing, Rosie." Bishop Jewell explained. "Before this is over, we're going to give these girls some property. We're going to give the girls money, and we're going to send you some money to help you take care of yourself. "

I will never forget the day we left. We packed our clothes in boxes, and we were driven over to the church. The name of the church was *The Church of the Living God.* Bishop Jewell, Bishop Harrison, Naomi, and Nettie Mae greeted us and hugged us. They put us in the very big fancy car that Bishop Jewell traveled in. She had specially built by chauffeurs.

The last thing I saw was my mother crying, but we would write her as soon as we got to Nashville. I couldn't believe that we were on our way. When we arrived in Nashville, the city was beautiful, but we couldn't believe our eyes when we drove up to the campus. The grass looked like carpet. The beautiful buildings were all made of brick. They took us on a tour of the entire place. It was just too much for us, and Maggie and I were giddy with excitement.

We came in on the weekend, so Bishop Jewell didn't put us in a dormitory. She took us to her big house, and let us live there with Naomi. She was an only child, so we became like her sisters. One of the things we did with Naomi was teach her how to harmonize. We would get in our room every night and teach her to sing.

We went to school on the next Monday. They had chapel on Mondays. Chapel was from eleven o'clock to noon, and then we would have lunch. Our classes were started in the evenings.

Maggie and I were called up to sing on our very first time in chapel, and we tore the place up. Nettie Mae played for us because she was the pianist. We had already rehearsed many times with her in anticipation that we would be called on to sing at some point in time.

The kids were ecstatic. We were the big poor kids on the campus. We were famous and popular. The kids looked up to us and honored us because we could sing like that. Instead of going through the horrors of the Twinsburg and Cleveland schools, we got the best treatment of any kids on the campus.

The schoolteachers and officials were very patient with us. They made sure that we were keeping up with the school curriculum and learning properly. They took their time with us and even sent some of the smarter girls to our room at night to work teaching us. They helped us to catch up to the grade levels we belonged in, and we were very happy.

Bishop Jewell would let us call our mama and talk to her. We would tell her how we were doing. We'd tell her how glad we were that she let us come down there and go to school. We told her we would be forever grateful to her because we were learning so much and doing great in school. We talked about how we were singing in chapel, and everybody liked us. We didn't have to fight, and no one bullied us. We made her understand the difference between the public schools in Cleveland and the Christian school in Nashville.

Naomi started singing with us. We would practice every night, and Nettie Mae would sit down at the piano and teach us new songs. We would go to the chapel, and they would set up the instruments, and we would rehearse and learn to sing with the band. Bishop Harrison would supervise our rehearsals making us practice every day, and we got better and better.

Naomi was a slight problem because she was shy and didn't like singing in front of people, but she could sing, and we kept encouraging her and telling her how good she was. We didn't lie to her; she did have a great voice, and she could really harmonize with us once she learned how to do it, and I knew without a doubt that we were going places.

We began singing in churches all over the place. Every time Bishop Jewell traveled, we would travel with her. We took our schoolwork with us. If the Bishop was going to be out for six weeks, the teachers would send our assignments for six weeks. They would place the lessons in folders according to the subjects that we were supposed to study.

Every home Bishop Jewell owned had maids and butlers, and everything you could possibly ever want was in those homes. We had the greatest food prepared for us. Anything we wanted was given for us to eat. They would keep our clothes washed and ironed, and we never touched them. They kept our hair clean, and every day we were made up to look cute.

We did our lessons at the dining room table, and the servants were given the job of making sure we were studying and finishing our work. Once we were back on the campus from a trip with Bishop Jewel, we would turn the lessons in and be graded.

One day, Bishop Harrison came to see us and told us we were going to make records. We were with Bishop Jewell at her church in Los Angeles, California. We had been practicing all evening at the church when Bishop Harrison made this announcement. We were going to get ready to cut some records.

We were going to a studio and make records. He said we were ready for it, and the deals had been made. We experienced for the first time singing in a studio and making a record. The sound coming back to us was fascinating. We really hadn't heard very much how we sounded together from the perspective of other people.

We made two or three records, and Bishop Harrison started taking them to radio stations. Every city we went to, he would take the records to the stations, and they would play them, and the listening audience was blown away. Promoters soon got involved and started booking places for us to perform. We were booked on famous shows with Sam Cooke and the Soul Stirrers, Lou Rawls and the Pilgrim Travelers, the Staple Singers, Mahalia Jackson, the Five Blind Boys, the Davis Sisters, the Harmonettes, the Swan Silvertones, the Dixie Hummingbirds, the Pilgrim Jubilees, the Sensational Nightingales, Archie Brownlee, the Consolers, James Cleveland, the Swanee Quintet, and this is just the tip of the iceberg of famous singers we performed with.

We were amazing, but the music industry never gave us the credit we deserved. Bobby Jones was a little boy out of Nashville, Tennessee. Albertina Walker, Shirley Caesar, and Dorothy Norwood are all famous singers. They sang with the Caravans and have known us for years. Everybody talked about them, but nobody talked about the Jewell Gospel Trio, and we were one of the hottest groups you can imagine.

We were the only group that brought music into the church. They never gave us credit for this. We should go down in history as the first Gospel group to ever grace the stage and auditorium with a four-piece rhythm band and a steel guitar. Every concert we gave in Nashville, Bobby Jones would be sitting there on the edge of his seat. You never heard them talking about that. They gave the credit to all the other artists that brought music into the Gospel industry, but you never heard then or now one word about what the Jewell Trio accomplished in the Gospel music world.

When we first started with our new style of singing, we couldn't get into the churches because they would say it was the Devil's music, so we could only sing in auditoriums and other entertainment centers back in that day. We couldn't get into the churches.

The only churches we could sing in belonged to Bishop Jewell. No other church denomination would let us bring our music into their congregations. We sang in a different city almost every week. We did everything live. We would congregate in the mornings at a radio station. Bishop Harrison would set up all the instruments, and the Jewell Gospel Trio would sing live. All the groups would sing live inside the studio, and the place would be packed.

We were drawing ten to fifteen thousand people to our concerts. We did concerts with Sam Cooke. Lou Rawls would bring his Pilgrim Travelers, and we would do shows with him. The Staple Singers were more our age, and we had the best time with them.

Bishop Jewell was very strict on us. I remember the Harmonizing Four. Bishop Jewell kept an eye on them. Instead of trying to molest us or do something stupid like that, they would teach us. They taught us how to act, and they protected us when we were on the road. They thought we were cute, and they would always tell us that if we were a little older... They told us we could sing, so we were the first Gospel group that made music history, and we still don't get the credit for it.

Nobody could follow us because we were that dynamic. We started a tour and were working our way to Los Angeles. We started the tour with the Fairfield Four, the Davis Sisters, and the Jewell Gospel Trio. The Davis Sisters were one of the best groups around. Ruth Davis could out sing anybody I ever heard in my life.

While we were working our way to California, we came through Shreveport, Louisiana. Everywhere the Jewell Trio sang, they had to put the seats back together. We could sing, and nobody could follow us. At Shreveport, the Davis Sisters were actually the stars of the show. We sang before them, and after we were done, they couldn't follow us. They were angry. They said it was embarrassing to get upstaged by teen-age girls.

We left Shreveport, and the Davis Sisters dropped off the tour, and that left the Fairfield Four and us. Now we were traveling with male groups and no females. We got famous and then started cutting records for Nashboro Records. We cut seven or eight records for them.

I was recently in Japan, and I was given a CD of all the songs we had recorded back in the day. I couldn't believe the greatest songs ever written were some of those songs. *Jesus is Listening, The Old Gospel Ship, Sin Is to Blame, Praying Time, Too Late, Ease My Troubling Mind.* We sang so many songs.

We grew into our teenage years with Bishop Jewell. We had gone to practically every city in the United States. There were only a few places we hadn't been that were in the more remote parts of the country.

As we grew older, we were starting to be mistreated. Naomi, her mother, and her father were in a different class than we were. The older we became, the less care they would give us. One of the first things they did was buy robes and make us wear them, so they didn't have to spend so much money on clothes. They would serve us potted meat and crackers for breakfast, and we were losing weight. In fact, we were becoming very thin.

Traveling on the road, it got worse and worse. I ran into Pervis, Mavis, Cleo, and Pops Staples one afternoon. We began talking about receiving pay for our work. I found out quickly that the Staples were being paid, and we weren't.

Things were really bad, and the conditions under which we were working were becoming more and more unfair. We weren't getting paid, and we weren't getting fed. We were hungry, and we had no enthusiasm for practice and learning new material for our act.

Here's a story I remember so well that illustrates how we were being treated. We were on our way to California, and I developed a very severe toothache. I complained that it was getting worse and worse, and I could hardly stand it. The Bishops refused to stop the bus and find a dentist to pull the tooth.

While I was on the stage singing was the only time I was not in excruciating pain but when we were finished, the pain came back, and I had to endure it and suffer. We had a group traveling with us. I don't know their names because we called them brother and sister. Sister was such a motherly lady. She was kind and friendly. Sister discovered my trauma, so she would hold the nerves in my tooth at night until I could fall asleep. I laid my head in her lap while traveling to try and ease the pain. I was crying I was hurting so bad.

We stopped somewhere in Texas. We stopped at one of Bishop Jewel's homes by the church she oversaw there. Segregation was so bad then that we had to travel in caravans to keep safe. We couldn't leave one person alone because of the danger from the Ku Klux Klan especially in the Southern states like North Carolina, Alabama, Arkansas, and Mississippi.

If you think cops are mean towards black people now, you should have lived back then. They weren't just bad; they were horrible especially if they saw a bunch of black people riding in a car at night. Bishop Jewell had houses at all the churches along the way that she was in control of. The houses were prepared for her entourage as they traveled through. These were safe houses, and all the quartets and singers traveling with her would stay in those houses. We had to time the trip, so that we would be arriving at one of the safe places before dark.

We never stayed in a hotel because there were no hotels that allowed black people. There were some black hotels, but they were more like transit houses, and the beds were down under the bar area. You couldn't sleep there because of the loud music and the thick smoke from cigarettes and cigars.

It is amazing how we had to travel and make way for the groups that are out there today, and they should honor us because we did the suffering and made the road easy for them. They are on our shoulders. We were the brick and mortar that kept Gospel music alive. They're standing on our shoulders and able to do what they do now because of the sacrifices we made, and we never get any honor for it. I am confident in myself, but it would be kind of nice to be recognized a little before we all pass on to the next world.

We were in the house in Texas after our performance that night. My tooth was hurting so bad. I was crying, and Bishop Jewell called me into her bedroom. She told me to come in there, so she could look at my tooth, and I can't tell you how badly it hurt. She told me to get on my knees, and so I did because she was the kind of woman that would whip the kids at the school with a rawhide strap if they disobeyed her. Some of the boys would be in the twelfth grade, and she would make them get on their knees, and she would whip them.

Bishop Jewel's husband was named Deacon Jewell. He was a very big guy, and he would tear your behind up worse than she did. Most all the kids would get a whipping at one time or another, but Bishop Jewell never whipped Maggie and me. All of this was going through my mind as I knelt by the bed. I thought she was going to whip me for crying about my tooth.

I was on my knees and instead of whipping me; she made me open my mouth. She took a tiny piece of lye; Devil's Lye was the brand. She put a drop of it on my cavity. By now the cavity was wide open, so she put the lye in there and then put a cotton ball on the cavity. She told me to bite down on it and when I did, I have never felt such pain. It's a wonder I didn't lose my mind. I jumped up.

"Come back here girl," she ordered.

I ran away from her to the bathroom. I pulled the cotton out, and then stuck my head under the sink and rinsed the Devil's Lye out of my tooth. I had to save my vocal chords. I don't know what the woman was thinking, but that Devil's Lye would eat up my vocal chords not counting the damage it would do to my mouth, my esophagus, and my stomach. I was old enough to know what damage something that dangerous could do to me.

My mouth did get sore, and I had little blisters for a while around my gums, but the tooth hurt worse than before. Bishop Jewell was undeterred. She told me that I should have left the cotton ball in, and the lye would have eaten up the rotten tooth.

You are making all this money off us, and you are going to barbarically treat my tooth like that. This is what I was thinking, and I was very angry with this woman I once idolized.

When we got to Los Angeles, there were two girls I met, who were doing a program with us. They had befriended Sister, the lady that let me lay in her lap and held my tooth until I could fall asleep, and Sister told them about my tooth, and how I had been suffering for days, and the Bishops refused to do anything about it.

Lisa was the name of one of the pretty girls. She had beautiful long hair and was by all counts a gorgeous girl. She belonged to a well-off family. She found her mother and told her about it. Now, her mother was just an older version of Lisa, and she called the police. She told them that I was being mistreated horribly.

The police pulled up in front of Bishop Jewell's house. They told us why they were there. Bishop Harrison overheard this conversation, so he pulled Maggie and I into the back room. He said the police are there to investigate something. He told us not to say anything. He told us to stay in the back room and don't come out.

"So somebody has lied on us," he said. They're coming here to see how we treat you girls, so you little girls tell them how good you're being treated. Tell them how Bishop Jewell is sending you to school and tell them about the school in Nashville. Tell them about all the good things she is doing, and that she would never do anything to hurt you."

I wanted to tell the truth so badly. I wanted to tell the truth, but I was scared. I was all the way out in California, and I was afraid of the Bishops.

The police called us all in. They talked to Bishop Jewell first, and she denied ever mistreating any of the children. All of them denied knowing anything about my tooth or ever mistreating one of the kids.

"Where are the girls?" The cop asked. "Where's those little girls? Where are they? We are going to question them."

The police brought us in the room and questioned us.

"You girls sing?" The cop asked. "You're the little singing girls everybody's talking about?"

"Yes sir," we answered.

"We want you to tell us in your own words how Bishop Jewell treats you; how this woman takes care of you."

"Just fine," I answered.

"Where's your mother?"

"My mother moved back to Alabama from Cleveland. She lives in Alabama. She couldn't make it with daddy living in Cleveland, so she moved back to Alabama."

"Well then," the cop said. "What are you guys doing way out here?"

"My sister and I are going to school at the Jewell Academy, and Bishop Jewell took us in when I was eleven years old, and we've been with her ever since. We sing on the road and make records."

"Don't lie to me," the lady cop instructed. " What about this toothache?"

Bishop Jewell made us sing for the cops, and told us to go to bed after they left. The next morning, Nettie Mae, Naomi's mother, woke me up and told me to get dressed.

I was taken to the best dentist for children in Beverly Hills. The dentist put me to sleep and extracted the tooth. When we were finished, Nettie Mae took us to a movie and then shopping for some new clothes. She was making up to me for the hurt they had caused.

The cops dropped the case but not without a stiff warning. They told Bishop Jewell that if anything else happened to the kids, they'd all be arrested.

CHAPTER SEVEN

You Never Really Wanted Me

After the meeting with cops, we returned to Nashville. Things were going pretty good. We were given a tutor, and put him on the road with us. The tutor's job was to keep us on the level we were supposed to be studying, and he made sure we had three good meals a day. The Bishops also gave us a little money, so we could buy things for ourselves.

Maggie was sixteen years old when our tutor, James Peoples, started dating on the sly. We weren't allowed to openly date, so they had to sneak around and see each other. We were in the cars together and in the band together.

Bishop Harrison was an ingenious person and a great business-man. I give honor where honor is due, and he was very good at running the finances of the organization. He bought us a limousine. We had one of the first limousines ever built. Bishop Harrison bought two cars and had a factory put them together, and we had the first limousine with our name on it. I remember going through the cities, and everybody would be standing along the roads waving to us because they had never seen a car that long.

Maggie and James were dating on the sly, and I was always the go-between. They would send messages to each other, and it was my job and responsibility to make sure the letters were delivered to each of them. When they were in the car together, they would sneak a hug and kiss when nobody was looking. The rest of us knew what was going on, but we would never tell on them.

My sister turned nineteen years old, and I was seventeen. We were still singing on the road and making records. Finally, Maggie decided to leave, so she went away and married James Peeples. She also went back to be with our mother, and she enrolled in Tennessee State University. The President of the University gave us scholarships. All we did was sing one time in the school's auditorium, and the President gave us a scholarship on the spot.

Maggie was the only one of the whole group of us, who actually did something with her free education. She had a full scholarship that covered four years of study and included everything she needed to complete her degree. Virtually everything was paid for.

Maggie graduated and became a schoolteacher. James Peeples was also studying and completed his Masters Degree in education. They moved over to Asheville, North Carolina and both of them got jobs teaching in a school. They left me with Bishop Jewell. Pervis Staples and I started dating a little bit, and he really liked me. We also dated on the sly, and Pop Staples started calling me his daughter.

Pervis had to leave the group and go in the Army. While he was in the Army, I wrote him every day, and we were talking seriously about getting married. During this time, Lou Rawls was still singing with the Pilgrim Travelers. There was a girl who took Maggie's place in the group. Her name was Shirley, and she was fond of Lou Rawls.

Lou Rawls was older than me. He was twenty-four years old, and I was only seventeen. He liked me, and I was a girlish girl. I always looked much younger than my age. I looked like a little girl.

Shirley was crazy about Lou. We called him Louis, and she wanted him badly. She was definitely in love with Lou. Of course I became the go-between because I was good at being a gofer. I delivered the correspondence between the lovers.

"Shirley says she really likes you," I told Lou Rawls one day. "She wants to get with you."

Lou had a very lackadaisical response, so it was obvious that he didn't have the feelings for Shirley that she had for him. I delivered a letter one day, and Lou wanted to talk to me.

"Look, forget Shirley," he said. "I don't like Shirley. I like you. I like you and want you."

"No, no," I replied. "I'm too young for you. Besides, I don't like you. Shirley likes you."

Lou was persistent. He told me never to bring anything from Shirley again. I agreed that I wouldn't bring her messages, and then he started hitting on me. He had this awesome Baritone voice. My God, how he could sing. I was developing a little and was dressing like a seventeen year old teenager rather than a little girl. I was cute and blossoming into a woman.

Lou kept hitting on me and kept hitting on me. He didn't know that I was still a virgin. I was outgoing and smiling at people, but I was innocent. I didn't know anything except I was just like my daddy. I would never meet a stranger. I laughed a lot and men thought I was flirting. I might have been flirting a little bit. I was just trying out my wings, but I didn't know a thing about men, and I didn't understand them at all. I knew they weren't boys, and that's about it.

Lou kept telling me that he was going to marry me. He kept putting on the pressure, but I told him I didn't want to get married. I told him that I was too young for him at seventeen, and he was twenty-four. I didn't stop teasing him, though. Every time I was on stage, Lou would watch me. He looked at me with those dreamy eyes and had that sexy look on his face as he stared at me. I began thinking that he really must like me.

I began thinking that maybe Lou wasn't all that bad, and the age might not make a difference. Finally, all I could think about was how Lou wasn't that bad at all. I liked to call him Lou even though everybody else called him Louis. Every time he would see me, he would call at me.

"Hey baby, hey baby, what you doing baby?" He would say.

I have to admit that my heart would melt. I was falling for him. I would never tell Shirley or Lou how I felt. I kept it a secret.

Shirley went to see Lou.

"Candi won't take any messages to you from me no more, but I want to tell you face-to-face that I really like you."

"Look, let me tell you something lady," Lou began. "I don't like you. Don't come up to me no more. Don't talk to me about liking me. I'm not interested in you, okay? You got that?"

Shirley was beside herself when she came back to our room. She got jealous when she saw me talking to him.

"You betrayed me," she said in tears. "You ain't no friend, you betrayed me." Shirley complained.

Shirley started bullying me, but I was going to have nothing to do with any bullying. I told her that if she kept up her harassing, I would beat her butt right in the church house.

We replaced Maggie with a girl named Betty. The group was now Naomi, Betty, Shirley, and I. We changed our name from The Jewell Gospel Trio to the Jewell Gospel Singers.

Shirley could really sing. We arrived once again in Los Angeles. We were going out there a lot. On the way, Lou got a message to me and gave me his phone number. He said he wanted me to call him as soon as I got to Los Angeles. When we got there, the first thing I did was call Lou. I told him I had to cut the call short because Bishop Jewell was in the house, and I had to be careful.

The next morning, Bishop Jewell, Nettie Mae, Bishop Harrison, and Naomi went shopping. Betty and I made plans. Louis would pick us up and take us over to his house. We needed to get down the street to a corner. We knew that the folks would be gone all day, so we lied and told Bishop Jewell we wanted to walk downtown and look around. She told us we could, so we went down to the corner where Lou would pick us up.

Louis was driving his old jalopy when he pulled up to the curb. I will never forget the old raggedy car he was driving. He drove us to his house. He lived with his mother, but she was a beautician and was working at her salon. We had the entire house to ourselves.

Lou put on some music and gave Betty something to drink. We weren't drinkers, but she took a little anyway. She was older than any of us, so Lou gave her a drink and told her to watch television or do something to occupy herself.

Lou put a record on his phonograph. The very first song he played was *Hold Me Tight and Don't Let Go.* "ooh ee ooh, this feelin' killing me, ah shucks, ain't gone stop until I get enough. I love you so, just hold me tight, don't let go, don't let go."

Lou took my hand and led me to the bedroom. I'm seventeen years old, and I'm a virgin. I was wondering what he was up to until he started kissing, and one thing led to another. That was the day I lost my virginity. I was so angry with myself for allowing this to happen. I didn't mean for it to happen. I ask myself over and over, *Why did you do this?*

"Why you do this?" I asked Lou. "I wanted to be a virgin when I get married."

"I'm going to marry you, baby. I'm going to marry you."

No you're not," I replied. "I'm seventeen, and I'm too young to get married. Why you do this? Why couldn't you wait until you married me?"

"I didn't know you were a virgin. I'm honest to God. I didn't know you were a virgin. I'm as surprised as you are."

"No you're not. You're not surprised. You're not surprised. You knew I was a virgin. Stop your lying."

"I didn't know, Canzetta, the way you flirt with men."

"I'm not flirting, I'm being friendly."

"Men don't take it that way," Lou answered.

Maybe I did lead him on, I thought.

I was too weak to walk. My knees gave out on me, and I couldn't walk.

CHAPTER EIGHT

I Wonder Will I Ever Get Over It
(I may get over it, but I'll never be the same)

I was too weak to walk. I was bleeding, and I was a mess. I didn't know that it would be so painful. I kept telling Louis to stop, but he kept going. After he was done, I tried to stand on my feet, and my knees buckled. He carried me to the bathroom. I was trying to regain my composure, and I didn't know if Betty knew what was going on. She knew, and I knew she knew. She was a grown woman, so she was aware of what was happening.

I cleaned myself up, and then Lou put us in a taxi and sent us back home. Before we left, he said that he was going to marry me. He promised that he was going to do it.

When we got into the house, Betty put me in a hot tub of water. These are some things I can never forget. I was so sore I could barely walk the next day, but somehow I pretended that everything was fine. It took a few days to get healed up, and then it was just a memory.

We did our final program in California and got ready to leave. I didn't see Lou after the episode in his house. The next time I saw him, we were booked together in a program somewhere that I have forgotten. Louis told me that he was going to send for me around Christmas time. He said when I was ready.

Lou wanted to know when I would have some time off at Christmas, but I told him that I was going home to see my mama. I always go home and visit mother at Christmas.

"Can't you come to California instead?" He asked.

"For what?" I answered.

"Because we're going to get married. We're going to Las Vegas and get married."

"You are serious?"

"Yes I'm serious. You come to California, and we're going to get married."

"How am I going to get there?"

"Here's the plan," he said. "When they think you're going to Alabama to visit your mother, you're going to get on a train rather than the bus and come out here. We're going to drive over to Las Vegas, and we're going to get married."

Christmastime came around, and I wrote my mother and told her I was going to get married. She wrote me back to find out that I was going to marry Louis Rawls, and he sings with the Pilgrim Travelers. She wrote back and asked me if I knew what I was getting into with a marriage so early. I told her when she wrote me again address the letter to Canzetta Rawls because that will be my name.

I boarded the train with no money. I don't know what I was thinking. I was on a train going to California with no money. California was a long way from Nashville, and I was hungry but couldn't buy food. Everybody was going to the food court, but I couldn't go. I didn't have a dime. I was sitting across the aisle from a woman who was looking at me. She had a little cute girl about seven or eight years old. I looked so young and traveling by myself.

The lady nicely invited me to come sit with them.

"What's your name, little Girl?" The lady asked. "Are you traveling by yourself? Come and sit with me."

She was a nice cute lady, so I sat talking with them and told the lady that I was going to California, and I was going to get married.

"Are you sure you're ready to get married?" She gently asked.

"Un, I'm not sure," I replied.

I told the lady my story, and I told her the man said he was going to marry me, so he sent for me.

"Honey, why didn't he send you money, so you could eat? You're not eating; you haven't been eating for a day, and I know you're hungry."

"I decided to wait until I get to California." I lied.

"No you're not," she said. "Come and go with me. Dinner is on me."

She took me back to the tables, and she paid for the dinner. God has always been such a wonderful God to me; even though, I did some wrong things, He always looks after me and takes care of me. That's why I know He's had His hand on me since the day I was born, and before I was born. He knew me before I was born, and He had a purpose for my life before I arrived on the earth. This lady I found favor with fed me twice while I was on that train.

I made it to California, and I got off the train. I retrieved my suitcase because I was given a case, so that I didn't have to pack my stuff in a box. I am thinking that Louis is going to be there to pick me up, but he wasn't. I stood there puzzled as to why he wasn't there to get me. I spotted a pay phone, so I called his house.

The first time I called him there was no answer. Now, I think I am stranded all the way out in California, so I called him again. This time, he answered the phone.

"Why aren't you here?" I asked. "I'm here in California, so where are you?"

"I'm home. Get a cab."

He gave me the address, and I wrote it down. He told me to walk out to the street and get a cab. I walked out as told, and the cab driver dropped me off in front of Lou's house and he paid the driver. I walked in, and Lou gave me a kiss, hugged me, welcomed me, and told me I was going to have fun.

When Evelyn came home from work, she gave me her bedroom and told Louis he better not be sleepwalking. She didn't know I came out there to get married. She thought I was only visiting.

Two days later, a letter came from my mom. It was addressed to Canzetta Rawls. Evelyn handed me the letter and asked,

"What's going on?"

She made Lou come in the living room and asked again,

"What's going on? She just got a letter addressed to Canzetta Rawls. Are you all married?"

"No mom," Lou answered. "We ain't married yet, but we're going to get married. We're going to Las Vegas and get married."

Evelyn glared at me. "Let me tell you something, little girl. You need to get back to Nashville and get with that group and sing. You need to finish high school. Louis ain't ready to marry nobody. Trust me, I know. I know he ain't ready to get married."

"Why you tell her that?" Lou asked showing his aggravation.

"Because it's the truth," she answered. "She's an innocent little girl, and she don't need to get hooked up with you."

I stayed there for two weeks, and every day he would say we're going to Las Vegas to get married, but we never went.

I share this one incident that happened while I was there. We were going to the movies one night. I didn't know that Lou drank very much, but he wasted no time getting drunk. I have never been around anybody, who drank like he did at that age, and he was a Gospel singer.

We were on the bus riding to the theatre. Lou had started drinking early that day, and he knew nothing about Los Angeles. I noted where we got on the bus, and we made it to the movies. Lou was really, really drinking a lot. He was so drunk. He was slurring his speech, and he couldn't walk without staggering. I was trying to hold him up.

We made it to the movie theatre, and he paid for the tickets. We made it to our seats, but it wasn't long before he said he needed to go out, but he would be right back.

He didn't come right back. He stayed out and stayed out and stayed out. I was getting scared because I thought he might have just abandoned me there by myself. I didn't know anybody in Los

Angeles except Bishop Jewell's church. I didn't want to go over there because she would find out I was with Louis Rawls. I couldn't risk them finding out because who knows what would happen after that?

Lou said he was going to the bathroom, so I went downstairs to where the bathrooms were, and I asked one of the guys coming up the steps if there was a man in the bathroom.

"Did you see a man in the bathroom?" I asked the stranger.

"Yeah," He answered. "I saw a man down there puking his guts out."

"How'd he look?"

"He's a dark skinned guy and kind of small."

"That's Louis," I said.

I went to the bathroom and knocked on the door. I called out his name.

"Louis, are you in there?"

"I'll be out in a minute," he replied.

"What's wrong with you?"

"I got sick. I just got sick. Let me get myself together, and I'll be back. Go on up to the movies, and I'll be up there in a minute."

I walked back up the stairs, and I waited. I wasn't watching the movie. I don't even know what the movie was.

Lou finally came up. He sat down beside me and said, "Let's go."

We left in the middle of the movie and headed back to the bus stop. We got on the bus and sat down. Within a minute of getting on the bus, Lou was sound asleep. He was sitting over there with his mouth wide open and snoring.

"Louis, wake up. I don't know where to get off," I said while shaking him.

"Wake me up when we get to his place."

"Okay," I said.

I was watching every street we came to. I went up to the bus driver and asked him to let me know when we were coming up to such and such a street.

"What's wrong with that guy?" the bus driver asked. "Girl, you need to get away from that guy. You look like an innocent girl, and he ain't no good for you."

"Would you just let me know when we get to our stop? I replied.

"Where you from anyway?"

"Nashville," I said.

"Well, you need to go on back to Nashville," he commented.

When we got to the street, the driver told me to wake him up, so I woke Lou up and told him we were on our street. We walked down the street to the house, and I went to bed as soon as I got in the house. The next morning, Lou kept apologizing for getting drunk.

I stayed around a few more days. I stayed for Christmas, and then I told him I was leaving on the train back to Nashville. I told Ms. Evelyn that I needed money for a ticket and to buy some food on the trip. She gave me fifty dollars, so I had plenty of money to get comfortably back home.

I got back safely, and Bishop Jewell never knew I went to Los Angeles rather than to my mom's house in Alabama. I took Evelyn's advice and wrote Lou a "Dear John" letter. I made it clear I had no intentions of ever marrying him. I told him I was going to do what I was supposed to do, and that was to finish school and get my education.

CHAPTER NINE

Lord I'm Depending on You to Take Me Through

When I got back to Nashville, I felt like a grown-up person. It was amazing how much I had experienced as a seventeen years old girl, and no doubt far above anything I should have known at that age.

Back in the day when I was growing up, nice young boys and girls did not have sex before marriage. We were taught that you save yourself for marriage. There were a lot more virgins walking around back then than are in the world today. I was so upset and disappointed in myself. My sister, Maggie, was a virgin when she married my brother-in-law James. I know this for a fact because they were in my mother's house when she consummated their marriage.

I admire her so much for protecting her virginity, and she never robbed herself of her self-respect like I did. I am not trying to put a bad light on Lou or anyone else. I am only reporting what I experienced, and I had a whole different attitude after my episode with Louis Rawls. I wasn't a virgin anymore, so I wasn't that hard to woo into a bedroom. I felt guilt from the experience I had with my uncle, but now I really wasn't a virgin, and I felt a lot of guilt about it.

I want to speak to the younger girls reading this book. Please get the stars out of your eyes. Stars are people with the same problems you have. The young girls chasing those stars disgust me sometimes. The groupies that came backstage with people like Cameo, and Earth Wind and Fire, and I saw how they would run behind those guys.

I was on the road doing tours with those singers, and I could see the girls running backstage trying to get to know these entertainers. It happened every night in every city. These girls are hoping to catch a star and have a one nightstand because that's all there would be.

It's not worth it. When you get older and look back over your life, you will realize that no man star or otherwise wants an easy catch. Save yourself for someone that is going to bring real meaning to your life, and you can build a quality marriage that will last for years to come. You can look back with a smile instead of remorse. Everything you do carries a price tag because nothing is free. You will pay for it, and sometimes you pay with your life.

I wanted to give this advice to the girls out there who have stars in their eyes. Remember they are humans. They're people just like you are. The only difference between a star and you is the job. The star entertains, and people believe they are bigger than life and put them on a pedestal. I believe everybody is a star. I don't know anyway to put this better than the song, *Everybody is a Star* by Sly Stone.

If you will look inside yourself, you'll find that purpose God has for you, and can build your life on what God has put in your heart. Don't try to hang onto someone because you are enamored with his or her accomplishments. Remember there are shooting stars, and there are falling stars.

I came back to Nashville and tried to resume my life. My sister had left and was teaching school. I would miss Maggie because she took the place of my mother. She always helped me to decide what was right and wrong and kept me in line. Maggie was gone, and now I was left floating around trying to make head or tails of what I was going to do with my life.

The first concern was the Jewell Trio. I was getting really tired of being on the road all the time. I had been to all the cities you would want to see as a young person and be excited about it. I had been to so many places over and over, and it was like wearing an old shoe. I had sung with the greatest from Aretha Franklin to James Cleveland. I had been in the greatest theatres in America and sang with superstars. Now, I found myself at seventeen years old bored with it all. I also wasn't getting paid, and that will put a damper on your enthusiasm about most things you are dreaming will make you a living. I went to talk to Nettie Mae.

Nettie Mae Harrison was a beautiful woman and when I say beautiful, I mean she was drop dead gorgeous. She was married to Bishop Harrison, and her daughter was Naomi. Nettie Mae was a perfect 38-24-38. She was the Dorothy Dandridge of her day. Every guy on the road, every quartet singer, and all the men in the groups we sang with were after this woman.

The way Nettie Mae walked was amazing because she drew undivided attention to herself. I used to imitate her. She would throw her hips one side to the other, and she could sing and play the piano. She would always say something before we sang. She could get everybody's attention.

I told Nettie Mae my story about Lou Rawls. Nettie Mae couldn't do right to save her life. She started slipping me out with her. The Ray Charles song, *She Ain't Going to do Right* fit Nettie Mae to a tee. She wasn't going to do right. She used to wake me up in the middle of the night, and she would tell me to get up and get dressed because we were going out.

I was seventeen years old and looked like I was thirteen years old. I looked so young for my age, and here I am running around with a woman in her thirties. I am trying to dress and put on some makeup to make me look older, but I couldn't get in the clubs. They would ask me how old I am, and I would tell them "I'm eighteen."

"You ain't no eighteen, you're not eighteen," they would say.

Nettie Mae was a person who would get in your face if she didn't like something going on. She grabbed me, and we walked in. She knew all the club owners, and nearly everybody in there. They yelled at her, "Hey Net!"

"Now Net, we ain't going to lose our license because of you bringing this little girl in here," the club owner cautioned.

Nettie Mae had planned for me to meet a man. He was a grown man, and he wasn't cute. He was ugly. He was trying to put his hands all over me. He kept telling Nettie Mae I was as cute as she said I was. I think the man was a pedophile. I was with Nettie Mae, and she wasn't going to let anything happen to me.

I decided that I was never going out with her anymore. I would fake sick, or do anything to keep from spending another night with Nettie Mae. I decided that when I turned eighteen, I was going to leave there. I was in the twelfth grade, and I went home. I was tired of it all. I was tired of the road. I was tired of not being paid. I was tired of being cheated. I was up there singing for the school, and they were cheating me out of money. They didn't appreciate me, so I got out of there.

I took the bus. I packed up my stuff and went to see Bishop Harrison.

"I'm ready to go back home, now," I told him. "I'm done. I'm done with this and the Jewell Trio stuff. I'm ready to go back home and see if I can find my way. I'll finish school there and spend some time with my mother. I don't know what is going to happen to me, but I wish y'all well."

The Bishop didn't say much but nodded his head. He sent a car for me, and I was driven to the bus station. When I got down to Hanceville, my mother had someone pick me up, and I was home for good.

Talk about culture shock. I had never in my life been in such a culture shock. I was looking at the Colony like the people in Cleveland and Twinsburg first looked at me. I talked better than they did. I didn't talk like them anymore. I became a city girl. I had better clothes, and I looked like I took perfect care of myself.

My mother had a TV now and a decent radio. I listened to the radio a lot and was constantly checking out everybody that was still out there on the road. I was being taking over by homesickness for entertainment. I missed it and longed for it. I thought I could be with Lou, and I should have married Lou Rawls. I would be living in California right now.

In the 2000's, I was in a show called "Say Yes." I was able to get with Lou again for no other reason than friendship. TBN asked Lou to co-host the show with me. After all the years of singing, he recently had released his first Gospel album. We did thirty-four shows for TBN. It was a great program, and I am glad I got to spend that time with him before he passed from this life.

I started school when I was back home in Alabama, and it was turning out to be very boring to me. I was also ahead of everybody, and that was a different experience for me. I had a young teacher, and all I was doing was daydreaming. I didn't have many friends because most of the girls were jealous of me. Every time I talked to somebody about my life, rumors would fly, and I would be accused of trying to take their boyfriends.

Life was miserable, and I didn't know what to do with myself. I was so bored. They had dances on Saturday nights, so I would get dressed up and go to dance. Boys would come around and ask me to dance, so I would dance with a guy, and then his jealous girlfriend would come up to him and slap him. I was thinking that this stuff makes no sense.

One Saturday, this guy walked up to me. He was a flashy dresser, and he had a 1957 Chevy. All the girls were chasing him, but I didn't find him all that attractive, and I wasn't paying any attention to him, but he was paying attention to me. He was always finding a way to be around me; even though, I gave no indication I was interested in him.

When I got home, all I could think of was the fact that at least he had wheels. I didn't have a car, and I didn't know how to drive, and I wouldn't be sitting around the house all the time.

The boy found out where I lived, so he would come by on Friday's and ask me to go to the movies. I would ask mama if I could go, and she would always tell me to go ahead. She would tell me every time to stay out of trouble, so we'd go to the movies. We would go by a little soda shop where they made great hamburgers and French fries. We would get a milk shake and sit and talk.

We'd be laughing with each other and having fun, and I started liking him a little, and it got to the point where I found him to be alright, and I couldn't wait for Fridays to roll around, so I could take off with him. Sometimes we would drive to Birmingham and hang around and drive back. Quite awhile went by before he started hitting on me.

At first, we were only friends. He had a great job in Birmingham, and I know he was thinking that he was spending a lot of money entertaining me, so I owed him. He started getting intimate with me, but I wasn't happy because I didn't think of him that way.

He kept on until the hormones were running high, and his testosterone was off the chart. Finally, I said to myself it isn't like this is my first time, so I gave in. We would start getting intimate, and then ride down to the dark side of the street near the park and drive back in the woods. We'd crawl in the back seat and get it on. *Let's Get it On, Oh Baby, Let's Get it On.* I was having fun, and I was using no protection. I wasn't thinking.

I was still so naïve, and I woke one morning, and I was so sick. I didn't know why I was throwing up. I would go to the back of the house and vomit. I wouldn't let my mother know. I was a high school senior with six months to go before graduation. I had been in school three months when I realized I wasn't having my period, and I didn't want to tell anyone that I thought I was pregnant. I prayed, *Oh my God Lord Jesus please don't let me be pregnant. I'm not ready to be a mother.*

I kept getting fatter and fatter, but I still wouldn't tell my mother. I told Joe. His reaction was really surprising. He kept smiling and smiling. He was glad.

"What am I going to do? I haven't finished school. I don't have no way of making money. Mama can't take care of both of us. I'm done." I complained to Joe.

I felt completely helpless and hopeless. I thought that I could hang my life up. I would not be able to sing anymore. It is so funny how when you come to that crossroads of life, when all hope is gone, there's nothing you can do. What was I to do with this problem? So, I didn't tell mama.

The news got out in this tiny community through this little old woman who lives there. We used to call her the old witchy woman because people said she could see into things. Her name was Miss Doney. I will never forget Miss Doney. I used to get so sick of her sitting on our porch talking about "I saw this, and I saw that."

I didn't know much about gifts like prophesy or being psychic. Miss Doney was sitting on our porch and kept looking at me funny. I was eating peanuts and throwing the shells off to the side. She is staring at me, and I heard her say, "uhm-uhm-uhm." It was creepy. Her eyes rolled back in her head.

"Miss Rosie, that little gal of yours is pregnant." That's what I heard her tell mama while I was walking in the house.

"Ah, nah, what, nah, she's not." My mother said.

"Yes, she is." Miss Doney said. "Watch her say, watch her say she's pregnant."

Miss Doney didn't only tell my mother, she told several other people. "This little ol gal of Rosie's is pregnant."

The word was all over the place that I was indeed pregnant. People would see me coming, and the girls would laugh and sniggle and talk among themselves. They were so glad I got caught.

I was getting bigger and bigger and one Sunday after church, Mother asked me if I was pregnant. We were cooking greens, and I was washing the turnip greens.

"Let me ask you something," my mother said. "People are talking about you being pregnant. Tell me the truth."

"Yes ma'am, I am," I replied nervously.

"Well, we got to get you to a doctor and get you some care."

I thought mama would blow up, scream at me, and call me names, but she didn't. She was the best. I can't explain the love my mother showed me during that time in my life without tears coming to my eyes. I was so afraid for her to find out. She grabbed me and hugged me, and I remember crying in the water of the greens I was washing.

"What am I going to do mama?" I said while boo-hooing.

"Well girl. You just going to go and have this baby. Just have the baby. Oh no, go on and have it, and it'll get taken care of. God will help you take care of this child."

I think mama was happy that I was stuck with her because everybody else was gone except my brother, Robert. He was still hanging around.

"You're going to be alright; I'm right here with you," my mother said as she hugged me.

I went to see Dr. Richards. He was from California and moved his office to Cullman, Alabama. At that time, they had "white" and "colored" waiting rooms. Dr. Richards had no such nonsense. He refused, and everybody waited in one waiting room. He maintained he would never fall for that segregation stuff.

Dr. Richards walked into the waiting room, put his arms around me, and walked me into his office. I was the only one he would do that for. The white women waiting in the room would stare at us saying, "huh,huh,huh."

"Is something wrong, ladies?" Dr. Richards said as he noticed the ladies' reactions.

The ladies would turn and look at their magazines or act nonchalant at being caught. Dr. Richards took such great care of me. He made sure I had all my vitamins and minerals. He did blood work, and all that was needed to give the baby and me the top care possible.

My boy friend, Joe, came to the table. He paid all the bills. Every time I went to the doctor, he paid the bill. He found out how much it would cost to get the baby delivered, and he started making payments towards it and saving up the money. He also saved up the money to pay Dr. Richards. Sometimes the Doctor would not charge me for a visit.

"You know what? You got a lot going for you," the Doctor said to me one day.

I told him all the stories about my singing and traveling.

"Don't let this stop you. Keep doing what you're doing. You're having a baby, and people have babies all the time. You're not the first that's had to deal with some adversity, you know."

I stayed in school, and the time for graduation came. I was walking down the aisle in my gown with the little hat and tassel. I received my high school diploma, and I was done with high school.

My sister and her husband came down and said that I should put the baby up for adoption and stay in school because I had a full scholarship to college already paid for at the Tennessee State University.

One of the teachers from the Jewell Academy wanted the baby if I wanted to let it go for adoption. I knew she was a good lady because she was one of my teachers. Arrangements were made for the baby's adoption, and for me to go to college. I was told again and again while making up my mind that I didn't have to accept the responsibility of being a mother right now. I could go on with my career.

Marcel was born in September. I went into labor while sitting on the porch eating peanuts, and the pains started coming. I had no idea what was going on. My mother and I had been out to the bean patch, and every time I bent over, I had this excruciating pain in the middle of my back. I had never experienced pain like that. I cried out to the Lord and asked him to stop it.

"Mama, I'm hurting," I complained.

"What?" She asked.

"I'm hurting, mama."

"Where's it hurting?"

"It starts in my back and comes around my stomach."

"You're in labor."

Molly, who was our neighbor and our cousin, lived up the street. She was the go to person in the Colony. She was always at the house and always telling me things I should be doing like how to conduct myself. She had told my mother that when it was time for me to go in the hospital, she would take me.

I'm sitting on the porch eating peanuts, and the pain got worse and worse and worse. I went in the house and thought I had started back on my period. They call it the S-H-O-W when you're going into labor. I told my mother.

"Oh, call Molly, call Molly," my mama screamed.

Molly was there in a flash and took me to the hospital. They put me in a private room. In high school, there were two students that were pregnant – Bertha Strong, my high school teacher, and me. We were all having our babies at the same time.

My mother was sitting by me and holding my hand. The pains were getting much worse. During those days, they gave you Ether to relieve the pain. A mask was placed over your nose and when you breathed, it put you to sleep. They gave you nothing else. That didn't stop all the pain, so you had to bear it until you got into the delivery room.

Dr. Richards came and gave me an examination to see how many centimeters I was. I didn't know what it meant; I was in a hurry to get it over with. I was in there all night and at about 7:30 a.m. the next morning, Dr. Richards came into my room.

"Okay, you're ready to go. You ready to have this baby?" the Doctor said.

"Yes, please get it out of me." I yelled. "Get it out of me."

We got into the delivery room, and they put Ether over my nose, and I didn't know anything else until I woke up to a bouncing baby boy. He was cute, and I mean cute.

"I wish Ersey was here to see this," my mother said. "This boy looks just like Ersey."

"What?" I asked in amazement to her comment.

Joe is dark skinned, and I am a little light complexioned, but my daddy was almost white. My baby boy, Marcel, was born with blue eyes.

"Lord, look at this pretty little baby boy with blue eyes," my mother declared.

Ha! I wasn't about to give up this baby. No way. I was released and went home after two or three days. Joe came up to the hospital to see the baby, and he was delighted, so he asked me to marry him.

"I'm not ready to get married," I said. "I don't want to marry nobody. I am just going to raise this baby by myself. Mama will help me. She said she would."

Joe's sister is Mary Lee, and his brother's name is Earnest. His dad and mom are Elder and Sister Williams. They came to see the baby. They took my mother into a room and started trying to convince her that Joe and I should get married. That would be the proper thing to do.

They made all my future plans without my consent. Here we go, making all my plans. It wasn't unusual for people to be making plans for my life. I fell into this thing because the Elder convinced my mother to convince me that it was time for me to get married because I couldn't raise the baby by myself, and the boy needed a mother and a father.

I agree with this philosophy one hundred percent, but it has to be the right father for the child. The father and mother have to be together in all the right ways. It is not just two people having a baby that consummates a marriage. They kept on me trying to convince me. Joe was bringing everything I needed, and Mary Lee brought clothes. Elder and Mrs. Williams brought all kinds of things to the baby. They brought the crib for the baby. It was amazing how nice they were to me.

When the baby was six weeks old, I was convinced. My mother told me that I might as well get married because she wasn't able to take care of me any longer. She literally backed out of taking care of the baby and me, so that was the sign I should get married.

I felt like I had no other choice, and I knew that was a horrible way to enter that sacred of a relationship. I always thought you should love the person you were going to marry. It's too bad that some girls get into this kind of predicament, and then have to settle for whatever they can get.

Listen girls, stay in control of your own life. My problem was other people were always in control of my life. From the very beginning they were, and what you learn to live with becomes very normal to you. Don't allow other people to run your life. Run your own life, and you know whom you are. Ask God for your purpose and stick within that purpose regardless of what other people may tell you. People can have all kinds of ideas for your life, and they can't run their own lives. This is only a gentle word of advice.

CHAPTER TEN

Freedom Is Just Beyond the Door

I can't forget the day after they talked me into getting married to Joe. I really didn't want to get married because my heart wasn't *in* it. I love Joe, but I wasn't in love with him, and I think he knew that. He became angry and bitter because of it. I could understand his feelings because somebody is just putting up with you, and there's no foundation to build your life on, but it didn't have to end like it did.

If Joe had been nice to me, maybe love would have begotten love. If a person doesn't love you, you can always treat them with love and respect, and the sweetness and kindness may draw the other person to you. They may have no choice but to love you back.

There's a song that says: *I'm Gonna Make You Love Me, oh, yes I will, yes I will. I'm gonna make you love me, oh yes I will.* If it takes bending over backwards to treat a woman with kindness and love, she won't be able to help loving you back. There's no way she won't. She would be pretty stupid not to love you if you are treating her with kindness, and you make her your queen.

You men have to treat a woman like fine China, and her every wish is your command. There is nothing she won't do for you. Joe and I would have been together to this day if he knew how to treat me.

It was on a Saturday that my mother told me to get married that day. Molly went with my mother and me, and my sister-in-law, Mary Lee, was with us. I wore an orange skirt and blouse. You weren't supposed to wear your blouse outside your skirt back then like they do today, but I didn't tuck in my blouse. I wore a pair of shoes with a buckle, but I didn't buckle them. I was dressed exactly how I felt. I wear my feelings on my sleeve, so people have no trouble telling when something is really wrong with me. They all knew my heart wasn't in this marriage. I had a baby with this man, but I was struggling with my heart.

Joe and I got married, and we didn't have a house. We went to my house and packed up my stuff. I didn't have a lot but with the baby's things that had been bought for him, it took two cars to carry all the belongings. The baby's bassinet took up quite a bit of the room. I was taken to live with Joe's mom and dad down in Warrior, Alabama. When I got there, they were so sweet to me. They welcomed me into their home.

Suzie Mae, who we call Miss Madea, cooked us dinner. She was Joe's mother, and she made some of the best cabbage I've ever eaten in my life. She taught me how to cook cabbage like she made it. She could also cook cornbread like nobody's business. You could make a meal out of her cornbread it was so good. She could also fix pumpkin better than any I had ever eaten. I was not particularly fond of pumpkin until I ate Madea's recipe. I wish I had kept it through these years.

These people were faith-based. They believed in divine healing and were healers. It was wonderful how they took me in and nurtured me. I have never felt more at home than they made me feel.

I was married about two weeks before I discovered and met the man I married for the first time. He was like a masked man who took off his mask and became the person he really was. How he turned from loving and kind and doing everything he could for me into another person is a mystery I will never understand.

When we were coming home from the hospital, it was raining, so Joe picked me up and carried the baby and me into my mother's house. He was so helpful and always made sure the baby had milk. He was wonderful, and then all of a sudden he turns into this dark person. I don't know what it was that came out of him, but it was a demon or something from the dark side of the world.

The appearance of this other person I did not know brought confusion and pain, and it was all such an unnecessary period of my life. I thought I had been mistreated before in certain places growing up, but I had no idea what was getting ready to happen to my life.

The first incident between us happened when he started accusing me of having relations with his brother that lived in the house. There was a lady, Ms. Vera, who he used to run into over at the juke joint. She started the rumor and put the idea in Joe's ear.

It's uncanny how people can get into your marriage and your life and destroy it for no good reason at all other than the love for pure gossip. Impure ideas come off the top of their heads, and they can destroy you with just an evil suggestion. Whether we know it or not, it's the Devil making those suggestions, so we can overcome him by not listening to what he has to say. He doesn't have any power, and we forget that sometimes. If we are stupid enough to listen to what he has to say, then we can get into a world of trouble. This was the recipe that started the downward spiral in our marriage.

"What are you doing over there?" The lady asked him. "You just got married. Don't you know that you're setting up that pretty little wife of yours at home with your brother? I notice he's not going nowhere because he's always at home with your wife, and you're over here with all the rest of the guys hanging out. You better get home to our wife cause, huh, you know, things happen, life happens."

Joe took that as serious as serious could be, and it set up a precedent in his life from that day forward. He came home that night and started accusing me of being with his brother when he was away from the house.

"What are talking about?" I asked him. "I'm married to you."

He would call me all kinds of names. He would come home and curse me out and tell me what he would do if he ever caught me cheating on him. It got so bad that I couldn't even go outside the house. I couldn't do anything with anybody. He would accuse me of cheating with every man that came to the house. He was insanely jealous, and it was the craziest of times, and the beginning of abuse.

There were many times when he would curse me out for no reason, and many times I would be coming out of a store, and he would call me a "ho." He would call me all kinds of names, and I became so frightened of him that I would literally be shaking from fear. The only time he was ever nice to me was when were dating, and when I was pregnant.

Six months after Marcel was born, I got pregnant again so fourteen months apart. I realize that older people know things younger people aren't aware of. When I was trying to nurse Marcel, he wouldn't nurse. I was dumbfounded.

"Taste your milk," my mother-in-law told me.

"What?" I said.

"Taste that milk."

I would taste the milk. I was breastfeeding, and I wasn't having a period, so that was nothing unusual because some women don't resume their periods while breastfeeding. I didn't know I was pregnant. I didn't even realize I could get pregnant.

"Is it salty?" My mother-in-law asked.

"It is," I answered.

"I'm going right now to get some Similac because you're pregnant."

I was pregnant again for real, and it was a bad one. It was worse than the first pregnancy. I couldn't go anywhere. Joe would come homework, and he would drive by the house several times. He worked for NAPA and drove a truck. When he came in the house, he would talk to me any way he wanted, which was mostly cursing and accuse me.

We did go to church. I had learned to play the piano, so I started a choir. They never had instruments before at our church. They mainly kept time to the music by handclapping and tambourines. When I joined the church, they told me I had to get the Holy Ghost. Elder Williams told me that I couldn't play the piano in the church until I got the Holy Ghost.

"Do you have the Holy Ghost?" Elder Williams asked me.

"I don't know what that is," I answered honestly.

"Well, you going to tarry," he said.

Elder Williams started me tarrying for the Holy Ghost, and I was at the altar a lot waiting on the Holy Ghost. They had me calling on Jesus.

"Jesus, Jesus, Jesus, Jesus," I would call.

I called on Jesus so much that my throat got so dry it was uncomfortable. I would start coughing and gagging, and I was about to throw up.

"That's it!" They shouted. "Them Devil's coming out, them Devil's coming out!"

"Jesus, Jesus, Jesus, Jesus," I said faster and faster. The faster I said "Jesus," the closer I got to receiving the Holy Ghost.

I finally got smart. I got tired of calling on Jesus until they said,

"Now you know when get the Holy Ghost, you'll be speaking in tongues. You gonna speak in tongues. You gonna speak in tongues."

Oh, Jesus, what is speaking in tongues? I was thinking.

I started speaking in tongues, and I got the Holy Ghost. I heard other people speaking in tongues, so I listened to them, and then I started. I listened just long enough to hear how they sounded, and then I took off speaking. I was so tired of calling Jesus because it looked like Jesus never was going to come, so I started talking like they were.

"She got it, she got it, she got it," they shouted.

Yeah, I had a ghost, but I didn't know how holy it was. I went on with them for along time, and it eventually got real to me. It got real because Elder Williams was really sincere with what he believed. I saw a lot of miracles happen in his ministry.

The Elder was a tall man and before God called him into the ministry, he was a drunk. His wife was a sweetheart. She really was a beautiful lady. At that time, A.A. Allen was finished in the ministry, and it Katherine Kuhlman and Oral Roberts that had come to the top that believed and preached pure miracles. They didn't believe in going to doctors and dentists. They didn't believe in medicine – they believed God would heal everybody. If you would go to the doctor at that time, they would discipline you, and put you out of the church.

People really got healed. I witnessed the healings for myself, and really got to know the Lord; even though, I was a little hypocritical at first. I started growing in the Lord, and began to see God move in a lot of ways that I never saw Him move before. The Scriptures came alive to me.

My choir at church was sounding very good, and I was rehearsing with the choir. There was a man there that I will call Brother John. He had a wife whose name was Lauren. They had just gotten married, and we would hang out with all the time.

Joe started accusing me of messing around with Brother John.

"Poor, poor Sister Lauren," he would chime. "I feel so sorry for her because I see how you be looking at Brother John every Sunday. You be looking at him. Y'all peeking around the corner at each other, and I see you. You think I'm crazy, don't you? You think old Joe crazy."

You are nuts, I'm thinking to myself. I never told him that because I was afraid of a backhand slap across the head, but I thought he was a nut case. I was totally innocent. I wasn't doing a thing, nothing. I was trying to do everything right. I would cook Joe's dinner and bring his plate of food to him. I washed his clothes. I was doing everything my mama taught me a good wife should do and be.

You can't appreciate a good wife unless you are a good husband. I have been with several guys, and I've been married several times. I never had a husband because none of them knew how to treat me. I know how to treat a husband and be a good wife.

After Marcus was born, I had another miscarriage. I got pregnant with Terry about six months after the miscarriage. After Terry, I had my daughter Cassandra. I wanted a baby girl so badly. I had three boys, but I wanted this little girl. I always wanted a girl, so I kept trying.

My little girl finally arrived. During those times, nurses would come to your house. All the poor people went to the clinic. We were still poor, so I went to the public clinic. A nurse from the clinic would come by to check on the baby and me. I had told her when she was coming and checking on Terry that I wanted a baby girl so badly.

"I tell all my patients this," she said. "If you want a little girl, take a vinegar douche right before you have relations with your husband."

"What?" I said in disbelief.

"Take a vinegar douche, so you'll kill some of that male sperm, so more of the female sperm can live. Try that, and see if it don't work."

I did the vinegar douche and sure enough, I had a baby girl and named her Cassandra. I was so proud of her. She was my boo-boo.

The married life kept getting worse and never got any better. I kept rehearsing with the choir, and Joe kept accusing me of wanting Brother John, and sometimes he would get crazy. We were coming from church with our three boys, and I was pregnant with Cassandra. The route we drove to church went through the mountains, and we had to go around these steep curves through Hayden, Alabama and through Blount Springs, Alabama. The whole route was nothing but mountainous roads and scary curves.

Joe was so mad at me because he said I was "making eyes" at Brother John that he driving around those curves like it was Indy 500 day. You could hear the tires squealing, and the kids were screaming from the back seat they were scared half to death.

"You done lost your mind!" I yelled. "You're gonna kill us all."

"I don't care if we do die," Joe commented. "I don't care what happens to us. You just a ho. You just a ho. You just a no good so and so ho. That's all I got is a ho."

"I'm not doing anything, Joe, " I said. Nothing's wrong. I'm not cheating on you. "

We made it home, and we were nervous wrecks. *Lord, how in the world am I going to do this? I can't live like this. This is crazy. I can't. I got three children, no I can't. I'm really in bad shape. I got three kids, no job, and only a high school education, and I'm not singing.* These thoughts dominated my days.

We were living in Warrior, Alabama but moved to Birmingham. We sold our little house that cost us seven thousand dollars for a brick home. Joe wanted to be closer to his job, so we moved.

I will tell you this story before we moved to Birmingham. We always went to Birmingham for a broadcast we had at four o'clock in the afternoon. It was a live broadcast, and Elder Williams would preach, and I would sing. I played the piano, and choir would sing.

After the broadcast, we would drive back to Warrior. This one particular day, we were ready to drive to the broadcast, and we had a miracle. Terry was two years old, and he was just walking and talking pretty well.

The broadcast was some thirty miles from our home. I was trying to get ready, so we wouldn't be late, and I was pregnant with Cassandra. Terry was hanging around, so I told him to go find his dad and let me finish getting dressed.

Joe had to go pick up some members of the church that would ride with us. Marcel, Marcus, and Terry would ride with us, and we would pick up another lady that lived around the corner. Her name was Shug, and she was in the choir.

Joe was getting ready to back out of the drive, and he didn't know that Terry had been following him. As Joe was backing out, all of a sudden he hit something. He thought he ran over our dog, he didn't. He stopped suddenly. He had hit Terry, and Terry was under the middle of the rear bumper. The bumper knocked him down. Back in those days, the cars had very heavy bumpers unlike the lightweight plastic bumpers we have and the automobiles today.

The car dragged him a little, and the skin was pulled off one side of his face. His face was oozing water. I tried to stand him up, but he couldn't stand. The sixteen years old boy across the street was yelling and screaming for Joe to stop. He saw the entire incident.

Terry was pinned under the bumper between the dip in the drive and the bumper of the car. Joe ran back there and saw Terry lying under the bumper. He picked that heavy car up and pulled Terry free.

I was devastated with my boy lying on the ground. He couldn't stand up. I went in the house and got a coat to put on him. I thought his back was broken. *Lord, these people don't believe in doctors. Elder Williams don't believe in doctors. What am I going to do? This baby has to go to the hospital.*

All of these things were going through my mind but all of a sudden, I heard this audible saying,

"I am going to heal him." When I heard the voice, I felt this supernatural faith and piece come over me.

"What do you want to do?" I heard Joe say. "What are you going to do?"

"We're doing exactly what we do every Sunday. We're going to the broadcast."

I wrapped Terry up in a blanket. I wiped his face and held him all the way. There was no seatbelt in the way because we didn't have them back then. I held him all the way to Birmingham. Terry was whimpering, but I knew in my spirit that God was going to heal him. I knew we were getting ready to witness a miracle. No one knew it or heard it but me.

I couldn't convince a soul that we were going to see a miracle. When we got into the broadcast service, the mother of the church held Terry while I sang, and I sang with so much confidence. I wasn't worried whether he would be healed or not; I didn't even think about it.

There were many hospitals in Birmingham, and all of them would have taken Terry in immediately and worked on him. I could have taken him to any hospital in Birmingham, but it wasn't the Will of God.

When I finished my song, the DJ working at that time was so angry that he was going to call the police.

"Are you all crazy?" He said. "That boy is badly hurt. He's been in an accident, and you need to get him to the hospital. I'm gonna call…"

"Don't you dare call nobody, you ain't in this," I cautioned.

I had that much confidence. When we got back home, all the saints in the church came to our house. They were praising and singing, praising and singing. Everybody was walking the floor praying, and they were around the bed praying. They were on their knees.

Terry was trying to raise himself up. He could only get part way up on one elbow, and he was moaning as the pain was shooting through him. He was whimpering, and my heart was breaking.

"God, you have to show up," I said out loud. "This can't last long. This has to be one of those got to be quick minutes of miracle minutes."

I am sitting by Terry, and he had calmed down while everybody left the house. Terry went to sleep. I stayed right by his bed. I was there by him praying all night. I would not leave him. If he moved, I was there. If he whimpered, I was there. I was rubbing him and consoling him.

Terry woke up. He screamed at the top of his lungs. He started writhing. His body was shaking all over, and he looked like he was going into some kind of trance or fit.

I don't know if you have this kind of faith. I don't know if I still have that kind of faith. I wonder how that kind of faith can be in a person. How can you believe God when all hope is gone? How can you believe when you see your child lying there almost dead and dying in front of you? How can you still know that God is going to heal the child?

I knew it. I have a knowing . I knew, I knew, I knew, I knew. I jumped up, put on my boots, and I have no idea what Joe was doing. I was doing everything in my marriage that the husband ought to be doing. I put on my coat and ran through the cornfield. It was about three o'clock in the morning.

Elder Williams lived about a half block from our house, and there was a cornfield between us. I put on my boots and ran through that cornfield. I used to call Elder Williams, "daddy."

"Daddy," I said, "Terry is getting worse, you got to come."

"All right, I'll be there in a minute," Elder Williams said.

The feature of our living room was a huge picture window. It was a nice little house with hardwood floors. Elder Williams was an old country man, so he showed up wearing his overalls. He sat down close to the picture window. We had a chair by the window, and Joe and I sat on the couch.

I had Terry in my arms rocking him, and he was screaming and yelling. Elder Williams just sat there and started having a regular conversation.

"We're really having a nice fall," he said. "Lord have mercy, looks like we're going to have a bad winter."

"Yeah, daddy, it's gonna be a bad winter," I commented.

I wasn't thinking about winter; I wasn't thinking about anything except getting this boy healed. *You gotta show up, Lord. You gotta show up now. I believe Lord what I heard from you.*

We sat in the living room talking about the service that night, and we talked about many things. Daddy started talking about politics, and how he didn't know who was going to win the Presidential election. All I could say to him was I didn't know who was going to win the election, but I hoped so-and-so wins.

My mind wasn't on anything but Terry. After a while Elder Williams looked at Terry.

"Boy, what's wrong with you?" He said. "Bring that boy over here."

I carried Terry over to the Elder and him on Elder Williams' lap. He started rubbing Terry's leg because he couldn't walk. I knew he couldn't walk because I had tried several times to get him on his feet, and there are plenty of witnesses to that fact.

"Boy, what's wrong with you?" Daddy said again as he was rubbing Terry's back. "Boy, you going to be all right."

Terry settled down to crying. You could see the expression on daddy's face. He was beginning to see a miracle.

"Heal in the name of Jesus, Elder Williams said as he hit my boy in the middle of the back.

I was looking out the picture window and suddenly it was like a lightning bolt came down. You could feel the electricity. That kind of energy can only come from God, and I felt tears running down my cheeks.

That energy ran into Terry's back, and he screamed and screamed. Elder Williams was laughing.

"Now get down from here and run over there to your mama," Elder Williams commanded Terry.

Terry jumped out the Elder's lap and ran and jumped in mine. I couldn't believe it. He had no pain; no more pain. He started talking, and all he could say was "eat." He was hungry. I went to the kitchen and fixed him a big mess of grits. I fed him and put him to bed.

"That boy's going to be all right," Elder Williams said as he was leaving.

I put Terry in his bed and pulled up the sides, so he wouldn't fall out, and he went to sleep. We all slept because we just had a visitation and when God visits your house, there is peace. We slept until about ten o'clock in the morning.

I woke up when I heard a noise coming from Terry's bedroom. He was jumping in his bed. I walked in the room and he was jumping all over the bed having the time of his life. He had a big smile on his face like nothing ever happened.

"Joe, come here quick," I yelled.

Joe had stayed home from work that day, so he came in the room, and we were dumbfounded. Terry's skin had grown back on his face. I picked him up, and I couldn't believe it. His skin was like a baby's behind. On his face where the water was oozing, and the skin had been pulled completely off the day before now was completely healed. Not only could he walk; but also he could jump.

I put Terry in the yard; so all the neighbors could see him. They were all mad at us, and said we were crazy. They were saying that they ought to call the police and have us put in jail for making that baby suffer like that. God wanted to show us how real He is. WOW.

The next day, I dressed Terry, and he went out in the yard with his brother to play. Cars were coming by our house, and they were lined up all the way down the street. You would think it was a circus going on. I looked out the big picture window.

"All these cars," I commented. "Folks are getting out of their cars and looking at that little boy."

"Which one of them boys got hit yesterday," a nice looking gentleman asked.

"This one right here. The baby," I answered.

"What happened?"

"God healed him," I said proudly. "He healed him last night."

Everybody around was coming to see the little boy that God healed. Everybody was coming, and they just couldn't believe it. The sixteen-year-old boy across the street had been telling everybody what happened because he witnessed it. It also made believers out of the bad talking neighbors, who had given us such a low rating on child rearing.

We went to church on Sunday, and we had so many people you

couldn't get in the door. People were standing outside the church looking through the windows. Elder Williams took Terry up on the stage to show him off, and the people clapped and clapped.

You cannot tell me that God is not real. I don't care what I do, how many secular songs I sing, how many hit records I've had, the one thing you cannot convince me of is that God is not real. This miracle sealed the deal for me. He is real in my soul.

Everything went back to normal. I kept playing the piano, and Joe kept accusing me of making eyes at other men. We moved from Warrior to Birmingham, so Joe could be closer to his job.

About a year later before we left Warrior, my sister-in-law came to live with us. My brother was fighting in Vietnam, so she came to stay with us. My brother asked me before he went back to Vietnam for his second term if his wife, Laverne, could stay with us while he sent enough money back for her to get her own place. They had a beautiful little baby girl, and her name was Leslie.

Laverne wasn't saved, and she had a TV. Elder Williams didn't believe in watching TV. They didn't believe in doing anything. We lived a strictly sheltered lifestyle in that church, and she brings a TV in the house. I was still playing for the church. We had bought a Hammond organ by then.

Marcel couldn't was about five years old at that time. He couldn't wait to tell Elder Williams that we had a TV.

"Daddy, granddaddy, granddaddy, granddaddy, guess what? We got a TV in our house," Marcel shouted.

Elder Williams sent for me. "This boy say y'all got a television over there," he said.

"Yes, sir," I answered. "It's not mine, it's Laverne's. She's my sister-in-law, my brother's wife, and he asked me could she stay with us until he got her a place. She's not saved, and she's got a TV."

"Oh, well I'll tell you right now you better get it out of there. I don't care if she's saved or not. You don't put the Devil's things and the Devil's box in your house."

"What?" I said in disbelief at what I was hearing. "Daddy, this is not my TV, and she's not saved. I can't do that. I can't put her TV out of my house."

"Well, you're gonna do something." He answered.

"Nah, I can't do it. You know I'm trying to be disobedient to you, but I don't think it's right to put her TV out. She watches TV. That's all she does, and she doesn't bother us. She closes her door and watches her TV."

"But them boys, them kids going to be affected and infected with that Devil stuff of the world."

"Elder Williams, they got to learn. I'm not trying to be disobedient."

Elder Williams wouldn't let go. He got hold of Joe, and tried to convince him to put the TV out of the house.

"I can't do nothing with that," Joe told him bluntly.

Elder Williams seemed to let it go for a few Sundays, but he was really cold towards me, and I knew he wasn't happy or satisfied. I also knew he had taken just about all he could.

Elder Williams stood up before the congregation and shocked everybody in the congregation. He told me to leave the church. He made an example out of me. If you get a TV, you're out of the church.

"Haven't I been a father to you?" He asked me in front of the entire church.

"Yes Sir," I answered.

"Why did you disobey me?"

"I'm not disobeying you."

"Don't you talk back to me," he said with a stern face.

You could hear a pin drop in the church.

"I'm not trying to talk back to you; I'm telling you that it's not my TV."

"Farwell," the Pastor said. "Farewell, farewell. You are out of here until you can obey me."

"Well, YES SIR," I said.

I walked out of the church, got in my car, and drove away. I was angry as I could be. I wasn't trying to show it, but the parking lot was paved with gravel. When I took off, my wheels threw gravel all over the front of the church.

Bam, bam, bam was the noise the gravel was making as it hit the building. People were scattering all over the lot. I guess I was pretty angry. I believe I had a right to be. I left the church, and I never went back.

"I ought to do what daddy told me to do," Joe said. He told me to beat you into subjection. You're supposed to submit. If you don't submit, then you should be whipped."

"You better not put your hands on me," I warned. "I will hurt you. Don't you ever put your hands on me."

I no longer was the pianist or an organist for the church.

We moved down to Birmingham, and I started playing for a church. They found out that I wasn't working, and I wasn't with the church any longer, so one of the pastors contacted me and asked me to come over and sing for them. Joe took me to the church, and I sang. After the service, the Pastor asked me if wanted a job, and I told him I did.

I was playing for the Baptist church on Sunday mornings. I was getting really, really mad at religion. I was disgusted with religious people. There's a difference between religion and a relationship. I was thinking there's a book in me, so I am going to write one called, *Religion Verses Relationship*. I have a lot to say about the subject. I really did enjoy playing for this church. The church was packed full every Sunday, and they enjoyed my music.

One Sunday, the pastor asked if he could talk with me after church. Joe came to pick me up, and he had the kids in the car with him. He was waiting outside for me.

The pastor told me to come on back to his office. When I walked in, he had this red smoking jacket on, and he had an alcohol drink in his hand.

"You wanted to see me Reverend?" I said when I walked in the office. "You want to see me?"

"Yeah," he answered. "I wanna see you. Have a seat. Would you like a drink?"

"No, Sir, I don't drink. I have my husband and my kids waiting for me in the car. You wanted to see me. What's on your mind?"

The pastor put his drink down on the desk. He walked over to me, grabbed me, held my hand, and then he put his arms around me and tried to put his tongue down my throat.

"Reverend!" I shouted. "What are you doing?"

"Most women would be glad for me to do this with them."

"I'm not most women. I'll see you later."

I never showed up at that church again. I stayed at home. I had no interest in church at that moment. I am talking to the Lord and asking Him what is going on? It seemed everybody I was around was stupid. Everybody was stuck in stupid. What kind of world is this? I began to see the world of different perspectives, different religions, and how messed up the people of the world really are.

"Would you be interested in doing some secular music?" My brother Sam asked me one afternoon.

"Secular music? Sam, you know I don't do that," I replied.

"Yes you do, and yes you will."

Joe was sitting there listening. Sam anticipating that Joe was going to get involved lit into him.

"Let me tell you something, man." Sam said to Joe. "I know how jealous you are, and I know how you treat my sister. But, I 'm going to tell you something right now. I will beat your ass if you ever lay a hand on her. I'm taking her. She's going to something for herself now. She's been doing something for you her whole married life, and I know my sister got talent. She don't have to sit around here and take your mess."

"Let's go," Sam said to me.

"Joe, you babysitting now," Sam said to Joe. "You babysitting today cause we're going somewhere."

Sam took me out of the house, and we went straight to the record store and picked up three records. We went back home. I had a record player that played 78 rpm. We started playing the songs. I learned *Do Right Woman,* and *Tell Mama.* Those were the most popular songs in those days by Etta James and Aretha Franklin. I've known Aretha since I was sixteen years old, and I've always admired her music. She could sing, and she is the best singer I've ever heard in my life.

I played the songs on the piano that Sam bought for me to practice on. I would play and practice singing those songs until I could get into my own comfortable key. I sang those songs every day.

"Be ready by Friday," Sam said.

"Okay, I'm ready," I said.

"Put something on that looks decent, "Sam commented. "Don't put on no more church clothes."

"Sam, I don't have nothing but church clothes."

"Well then, come on, and let's go to the store."

We went to the store, and Sam let me pick out a top. It didn't have sleeves, and I matched it up with a low cut skirt. Friday came, so I dressed up and went with Sam to the club.

A guy named O.J. was Sam's Masonic brother, and so they did some kind of sign Masons make to each other.

"You going to let my sister sing tonight?" Sam asked O.J.

"Your sister can't - she can sing?" O.J. asked surprised.

"Yes, yeah, you better believe she can sing. Sing better that them folks you got coming up here trying to sing."

"Well," O.J. said. "Sam, Sam…"

"O.J. trust me. My sister can blow, man."

"She better be able to blow. She ain't gonna embarrass up here, and make me lose my clientele." O.J. explained nervously.

I didn't even rehearse with the band because the song was so popular they were already playing it. The house band O.J. had was playing everything popular.

"I got a surprise for everybody," O.J. said from the stage.

At that time, I was known as Canzetta my real name and not Candi.

"We got a little girl here. Her name is Canzetta. What do you want me to call you?" Joe said to me.

"Call me Staton," I replied.

"Oh, her name is Canzetta Staton. Y'all welcome to the stage right now, Canzetta Staton."

"Can y'all play *Do Right Woman?*" I asked the band. "Put it in the key of F."

"Do you know your keys?" The bandleader asked.

"Yeah, I know my keys."

I sung *Do Right Woman,* and the crowd went completely crazy. I sang it just like Aretha. I am not saying I can out-sing Aretha, but

I sang Aretha's song in my own style. I always put my own style in any song I sing. I gave them a little bit of Candi Staton. They started clapping. They stood up and kept clapping and yelling, "more, more, more, more."

"Man, where did you find that woman? Where'd you find her?" One of the men asked from the crowd.

O.J. took me to the back of the club. "You want a job?" He asked.

"Yeah, I want a job."

"Can you be here Fridays, Saturdays, and Sunday nights? Learn some more songs, and come down here Thursday and rehearse with the band."

So Sam would come and take me to the club because he knew Joe wouldn't do it. Sam had a babysitting contract with him he couldn't get out of. Joe was so mad. He was livid, but he couldn't do a thing about it because Sam had a reputation of beating people up he wasn't happy with. He didn't play around and would knock the fire out of you. He would stand up to the Devil himself, and Joe knew it. Joe was genuinely afraid of Sam, so he didn't mess around with him.

When Sam took me to work, he would stay there with me, and then take me back home. Joe would be so mad and upset when I got home. He would accuse me and tell me what he was going to do to me, and how he was going to make me suffer for when I told him be better shut up or Sam would beat him up.

I worked my butt off and was able to go to the club and work without Joe bothering me too much.

I was working and doing my job, and the surprise of my life happened. Clarence Carter came to town.

"Canzetta, Clarence Carter is coming," O.J. announced to me.

I was listening to secular music then, and I heard Clarence Carter on the radio. I was breaking into the business, so I listened to all the secular songs. Clarence was supposed to come the next week.

"I got a girl here that's going to open for you, "O.J. told Clarence.

"No, no, no you don't," Clarence said. "I got my own review. Ain't nobody opening for me."

"Clarence, you gonna have to hear this woman. O.J. said. "This girl can blow. I wouldn't lie to you."

O.J. convinced Clarence that I would lead his act and sing before he came on to perform. I had to rehearse with Clarence before anything could be decided for sure. Clarence wasn't going to let any band play before him because they didn't have to. You don't have time to take down and set up two separate bands.

"She got to be at rehearsal before we get there." Clarence told Sam.

It was on a Friday and Clarence told Sam, "She better be here."

Sam came and took me to rehearse with Clarence Carter. I was in total awe of him at that time because he had such a big hit record. His huge hit Slip Away was out. He had a couple more songs, and he was really popular.

The Club only held about 150 patrons, but it was so packed with people that they were standing all the way around the walls.

"Alright, let's see what you can do," Clarence said to me.

"Can y'all play *Do Right Woman?* " I asked Clarence.

"I think we can manage that," he said.

"Can y'all play Tell Mama? Do you know Tell Mama?"

"Ha,ha,ha," Clarence laughed his classic chuckle. "I think we can handle that one too."

I didn't know that Clarence Carter had written *Tell Mama.* Of course he could handle it because he's already made a record call *Tell Daddy* before Rick Hall made the record on Etta James called *Tell Mama.* In fact, Rick Hall produced both those records that became mega hits. I was up singing, and Clarence was saying, "Tell Mama all about it. Tell Mama what you want."

After my show was over, Sam and I stayed to hear Clarence's show and stayed until it was completely over. Joe showed up during my performance. He got the girl next door to babysit, and he came on down to the club. I could barely perform because Joe was walking back and forth in front of the stage until Sam got him on the side and made him sit his tail down.

Joe had a gun on him. I knew things were getting bad, and I also thought things were going to dangerous before it was all over.

"You can really sing," Clarence said to me. "You sing like folks used to sing. Where did you learn to sing like that?"

"I sang Gospel in church, and I sang with the Jewell Gospel Trio, and I know Sam Cooke," I explained.

"Can you go on the road?" He asked.

"Well, no, I can't go on the road. I got a jealous husband, and he will kill me. I can't travel yet.'

If you get rid of that fool," Clarence said. "Give me a call."

Clarence gave me his contact information, and now there was a ray of hope is how I saw it. I thought, *Oh, my God. Yes, Yes, I got a way out. I got a way out. How can I get away from this man, Joe. I've got to get me a divorce.*

I stopped singing at the club. I went to United Records in Birmingham and got a record deal. We made a few records, and there is a rare edition called *You've Got the Upper Hand*. It's a collector's item in the music genre of Northern Soul with a white label and if you can find it, it's worth about thirty thousand pounds.

My record was doing pretty good. We were going to the radio stations asking them to play the record. We got some airtime in Birmingham. Alexander was a D.J. and he appeared in my life. He always was hanging around me. He called on me all the time to go places with him to sing.

Home life was terrible while this was going on. We had a girl, Janet that we brought down from Warrior to stay with the kids. She lived in the house with us. This allowed me to go and do pretty much what I wanted, but I caught hell every time I came home.

"I'm doing a gig over here," Alexander would tell me. "I want you to come over here and sing."

I would go with him and sing. There wasn't much money in it, but it was something to do. One night I had been with Alexander. I went somewhere with him, and it happened to be Valentine's Day.

Valentine's Day was my nemesis. So many bad things happened to me on Valentine's Day. Everything bad that can happen to anyone on Valentine's Day happened to me.

Joe came in drunk. He was stone drunk. My eighteen months old little girl, Cassandra, and I were lying on the bed. She was restless and couldn't sleep, so I brought her into the bed with me.

Joe came in the house. It was about nine o'clock p.m., and we had been watching TV. He came into the bedroom where Cassandra and I were asleep.

"I know you been with Alexander," he said. "I heard. You think I'm crazy, don't you?"

"No, Joe, I don't think you're crazy. What are you talking about?"

"I heard about you. You, you going with that nigga"

"No, I'm, What? Here you go again. What are you doing? You're always accusing me. What are you doing?"

I don't know why I went and said what I did. It was the wrong thing because I hit a rough spot. He grabbed the bed mattress and all and threw it over us. When he looked around, we were coming out from under the bed. My baby was crying, and I was trying to get the bed and mattress off me. I was struggling trying to get my baby out from under the mattress.

The baby stood up and started walking, and then Joe grabbed me. He grabbed my hands and put them together like he was going to handcuff me.

"I told you I was gonna kill you," he said as he cuffed one of my hands. "I told you I was going to do these things to you. Why do you make me do these things to you?"

Joe started beating me with my own hands. "I told your mother. She told me I couldn't put my hands on you, so I'm not gonna put my hands on you. I'm gonna make you put your hands on you."

Joe overpowered me with his strength. He beat me with my own hands until I was black and blue from the top of my head to the soles of my feet. He then started dragging me out to the car.

I'm taking you home to your mama," he exclaimed.

Interstate 65 was under construction coming out of Birmingham. They were just making the road. It was rainy and cold that night. I only had a nightgown on when he dragged me to the door. I think every piece of furniture was dragged to the door with us because I was hanging on for dear life.

I don't know what I was thinking, but all I could think of was that I had to get a coat. I had to get my coat and shoes, so I could run. I bolted for the closet, but he grabbed me and beat me again. I struggled, but he was able to put me in the car. He was trying to start the car while he was holding both my hands together with his free hand like I was in handcuffs.

I kept struggling and pulling and trying to get myself free from him. I finally worked myself loose from his grip. I got out of the car and instead of running down the road screaming, I went back towards the house. I had to get my coat. All I could think about was getting my coat and shoes because I didn't want anyone seeing me in my nightgown.

It sounds dumb. My life was in jeopardy, and I had to get my coat and shoes. I finally got them, and then I heard that same voice I heard that told me Terry was going to be healed. The voice told me that when I get to the ignition, get the keys and throw them away.

I got the keys out of the ignition. Joe got the keys, and I struggled but finally was able to get them out of his hands. I jumped out of the car and hurled the keys as far as I could down in the bushes.

While Joe was going through the bushes trying to find the keys, I went into the house and got my coat and shoes. The boys were asleep, and Cassandra was screaming. I couldn't take her with me. She came running after me screaming, "mommy, mommy, mommy." I told her I would be back.

I ran next door to my distant cousin's house. I banged on the door, and she opened the door and took me in.

"Janet, get my baby," I yelled, and she took my baby. "Janet, call my brother."

I don't know why I didn't call the police but instead, I told Janet to call Sam. Janet wouldn't do it. I couldn't figure out why she wouldn't, but I have a good idea.

I got hold of mama, and I told her that Joe just beat me up. The man of the house, my cousin told my mama that they've known all along how Joe treated me.

"Ms Rosie, we saw it. We saw but didn't say anything. You need to come and get your daughter and take her home."

CHAPTER ELEVEN

Too Hurt to Cry

The man my mother married, Brother Marsh we called him, was a great guy. He was a very strong man. He was an older man, but he had a lot of strength and an amazing old man. He had fatherly instincts.

Brother Marsh and my mother drove their truck down to Birmingham, which was about thirty to forty-five miles from where they lived. When they got to our house, they parked the truck. Brother Marsh had just taken a load of pigs to the slaughterhouse, and he didn't really have time to clean out the truck, so there was still manure in the bed of the pickup.

They were anxious to get to me to see how I was and make sure I was okay. Joe was still banging on my distant cousin's door and he was told that if he kept acting crazy like that, they were going to call the police.

When my mother saw the way I had been abused, she looked at me in complete shock at what Joe had done to me. Mama and Brother Marsh walked me back to my house.

Brother Marsh couldn't take it any more, so he grabbed Joe and pushed him against the wall and held him there. He was so strong that Joe felt his power, and knew there was sense trying to mess with this old man. Brother Morris started rebuking him.

"Man," he started. "What kind of husband and father have you turned out to be? You should be ashamed of yourself the way you have treated this little girl and these kids. You're no man. You're not a man. You're nothing. You, you know what? I need to take you out here and beat you down, and you need to be tarred and feathered and hung up in a tree somewhere by the way you've treated your family. This little girl didn't deserve this."

Brother Morris stood guard over me and wouldn't let Joe near me, so he couldn't do anything else to me.

I have been told that a streak of jealousy was in Joe's bloodline as far back as his great-grandfather. One of Joe's cousins on his father's side had to be committed to a mental institution. That's how bad it was. I personally believe Joe was mentally ill. People seem to sweep mental sicknesses like being insanely jealous under the rug. They know there's a pink elephant in the room, and everybody tries to ignore, but sometimes it can't be.

We got into the house, and I got the children dressed and put on their winter clothes. It was rather cold on this particular 14th day of February. I put their hats and coats on, and meanwhile Joe was emptying the drawers. He brought the drawers out of the dressers and dumped them on top of all the manure that was in my stepfather's truck. He was bringing drawer after drawer and screaming, "Yeah, take your kids."

Get away from me. I don't ever want to see you again. "Take em, I *don't ever want to see any of you again.." I was thinking all this to myself. These are your children. What kind of person is this? These are your children. What man does his children like this?*

We finally got situated, and I got into the truck with my mom and stepdad. I took pillows, blankets, and quilts and put them in the truck. I wrapped my little daughter, Cassandra, in blankets, and everything I could think of, I put over the boys, who were lying on top of clothes in the bed of the truck. They put their heads under the covers and got ready for the cold air to blow on them, and that's how we went to my mother's house.

We talked all the way to my mom's house. Mr. Marsh was very, very angry. He kept saying something was wrong with Joe that he acts the way he does. The more he talked about him, the more used and abused I felt. I was in a mental turmoil and almost a breakdown wondering how I was going to support this family by myself.

The bruises Joe put on me from my beating had healed on the outside after about a week. That didn't heal the emotional bruises and bleeding on the inside. I was twenty-four years old with four children to raise alone. This was a drama I didn't know how would pan out. I've always been strong, and I've been through times that would have folded up most people. Some women would have raced to drugs and become crack addicts or addicted to some other horrible drug. They would have put the kids in foster homes and said, "forget this. I can't take it."

God knew my heart, and He steps up to the plate when you're about to strike out gives you the determination and strength you didn't know you have. I had to become a mother and father to my children. I love them, and they were all I had. I couldn't let them down.

I walked around in my mother's house for months wondering how in the world I was going to survive. I looked for work. I called a lot of places and inquired about a job. I am not one to sit around doing nothing. I tried to get a job in Cullman. I used to work for some ladies up there. I worked for some ladies doing housework because there were people in the Colony who had jobs in the homes doing various domestic things. I worked at that job for a while and quit because I didn't make enough money.

I filed for divorce, and it took a month for it to settle and the marriage dissolved. Joe didn't contest it, so it was easy. The Court awarded me custody and ordered Joe to pay fifth dollars a month child support. That wasn't per child; it was total for all four kids. How sad is that? Twelve dollars and fifty cents per week per child.

Joe lasted three months paying his dues. That's all he paid. After five months scraping to get by living with mama, my brother, Joe, who lived in Cleveland and Louise, his wife, invited us to come up there and live with them until I could get back on my feet and my life in order.

My sister, Lily, also lived in Cleveland. She had four kids of her own and was on welfare. There are certain things you can't do when you're on welfare because the authorities come around periodically and check your living conditions. You can lose your welfare status if you have other people living with you and sharing the welfare.

Joe, my brother, sent a bus ticket for all of us, so we packed up and left. Mama hated to see us go, and she was so worried about us. Joe said he could get a job for me up there that would pay better than anything I could find in Alabama.

I landed a job at a senior citizens home on Euclid Avenue. When I went in to interview for the job, I had no idea how to make up a resume or fill out a job application. Look at my background. I was a singer with Sam Cooke and all those people on the road, and I sang in front of thousands of people, but I had no experience looking for a regular job.

I went into the home and honestly told them that I had four children to support, and I needed a job. I got hired, and it was really very hard work.

Older people in some of those homes get mistreated. I saw it first-hand where I was working. Some of the old people in there didn't even get visits from their families anymore. They were so lonely, so I took the talent God gave me and used it. I read to them during my breaks, and they started loving me. They started calling me Candi. They would say that I was the sweetest little thing – little Candi Cane. They wouldn't call me Canzetta because it was too much of a name, so I became Candi.

I would read the Bible to the folks, and I would read other books as well. When I was done working during the day, I would go their rooms and clean their beds and put on clean sheets. I would take them to the bathroom and bathe them. I talked to them, and they really loved me.

I had more work than I could possible do because some of the nurses there were mean and treated the patients very poorly. They didn't want them around. When the nurses were mistreating the old people, I could hear them calling me all the way down the hallway.

"Candi, Candi come."

"I don't want you to touch me," they would say to the nurses. "I want Candi to touch me."

I really did enjoy the work that lasted for a while, and the pay wasn't enough.

I was always off on the weekends, so my brother Joe and I would go out. I had time to enjoy myself a little and being only twenty-four years old, I wanted to get out of the house and away from work.

Saturday nights, we would go to the clubs. One Saturday, the band heard about me singing. My brother told them that I had been singing all my life.

"You should hear my sister sing," Joe insisted.

"Well then, tell her to get up here and sing," the bandleader said.

I went up on stage and sang *Stormy Monday*, and immediately the band wanted to hire me.

"Okay, what do you want from me?" I asked.

"We want you Friday, Saturday, and Sunday nights. That's all you have to do."

"Okay, I'm in," I said. "Let's do this."

They paid me fifty dollars a night, and back then that was real good money. That money was added to the fifty dollars a week I was making at the nursing home, so I was able to save enough money to get an apartment.

I never heard from Joe (my ex husband). He never tried to call me and never tried to see his kids. He never wrote to them, and he made it clear that he didn't care what happened to us, or where we were.

I stayed with my brother Joe and his wife for three months, and I had to get out of there although I appreciated their hospitality. Their little girl was mistreating my baby. She would scratch and bite her, and the parents really never disciplined her very much or made her mind.

I looked for an apartment and had in mind just what I wanted.

I found it on White Avenue near Huff. Huff was famous for gang violence and one of the worst parts of Cleveland. It was an easy place to get an apartment, but I don't know how we made it over there except that God was with us.

The apartment cost sixty-five dollars a month. It had two bedrooms, a little bathroom, and a tiny kitchen. It had a small eating area, and a small living room area. We had to pay the electric and gas bills so needless to say, I struggled.

There was a guy that worked with me at the senior citizen's home. His name was Hopps. I told him about my many struggles.

"I will help you," he said. "I will help you with the children. Let me move in, and we can share the rent, and I'll keep the children when you work, and you keep the kids when I work."

It sounded like a good plan, so I told Hopps, "Bring your stuff over and move in."

It worked pretty good for a while. He was kind to the kids. They liked him and especially, the boys. He would play with them and take them places like the park to keep them active.

It was all working until Hopps found out I wasn't interested in him, personally, and it all started to fall apart. He would sometimes leave the children in the apartment by themselves. I was ready to give up, throw in the towel, and go home.

"I can do better at my mother's house," I complained. "Maybe I can leave my kids with my mother and go to Nashville, or go somewhere and find me work to do."

I was thinking of calling the Jewell Academy and getting back with the group. I didn't know what I wanted to do.

My sister, Lilly, kept trying to get me to apply for welfare, but I saw what welfare had done to her, so I refused. I didn't want to get too satisfied while stuck in a rut. I am not putting people down that really need it, but I'm speaking personally. It wouldn't have been good for me. It would have messed me up. My dreams and aspirations were much higher than that. I thank God for welfare that helps people when they're down, but I would have gotten satisfied and settled because of the rules and regulations that apply to those programs.

While I was thinking about moving back to Alabama my sister, Maggie and her husband James, came home from Spain where James was working on his Doctorate in Foreign Languages. They had called mother, and she told them I was in Cleveland. My sister told them where I was living.

They came to Cleveland to see how I was living. They knew that I had divorced Joe, and I was trying to make it with the kids on my hands. They showed up about three o'clock in the morning, and I was thinking about leaving Cleveland. I was just about to give up.

Maggie and James could not believe my living conditions. They went in the bedroom and checked on the children. They were all asleep. We were really in some sad living conditions. The saddest part of all was created by the environment where we lived.

My boys were getting into fights with the kids that were bullying them. They had to run for their lives. One day, Marcus came home from school, and I didn't understand the commotion that was going on.

I was on the three o'clock to eleven o'clock shift and was about to go to work, and I saw Marcus. He was getting a knife out the drawer, and I could see that he had been cut. A boy had cut him with a bottle, and his leg was bleeding. He grabbed the knife and said he was going to kill somebody.

"Oh, no you're not," I told him. "Put that knife down. What's wrong with you boy? You're not killing anyone."

It was getting rough in Huff. My boys would have eventually ended up in a gang or something even more devastating. Marcus would not have been the nice, wonderful, great drummer that he is today if I had kept him in that environment. Environment has everything in the world to do with the welfare of a child. Sometimes you have to take them out of the place you live in order to save the child.

Marcus has worked with Tyler Perry, and he's played drums with everybody in the R&B world. He's worked with the Pointer Sisters and many others. He would not be who he is today if I had not moved him out of those living conditions.

Maggie and I sat at the table with James trying to figure out what to do with us. I thank God now for my family. Families are everything. Friends are great, and sometimes they are faithful, but you can always depend on good family members. If you don't have anything else in the world, you have your family.

We talked about placing the children in homes, so the next morning when we woke, I didn't go to work. I called in sick. We talked all day, and we called Aunt Lula, and she said she would take Terry. Betty, her daughter, would take Marcus. We called Elder Williams down in Alabama, and he said he to bring Marcel, and he could stay with them until I got on my feet. We took Cassandra with us, and we piled in their car along with some clothes. I left the apartment. I don't know what happened to the furnishings, and I couldn't care less. We got in the car and drove to Nashville.

I kept the kids in the daytime while Maggie and James taught school. At night, James would take me to the local clubs to work. I worked in the smaller clubs while I waited to enter the fall classes of Vanderbilt University to be trained as a Registered Nurse. I wanted to be a nurse. It's what I always wanted to be. It was summertime, and it wasn't time for fall classes.

James, Maggie, and I were riding in downtown Nashville, and we saw a placard. Clarence Carter was coming along with Bobble "Blue" Bland, Johnnie Taylor, Denise LaSalle, and the Lord knows who else. They were all R&B singers, so we stopped at the auditorium, got the date, and bought the tickets.

The date finally came. I was giddy with excitement. I going to try and go backstage. Once we got in our seats, Maggie and I were talking and trying to figure out how to get backstage.

"How can we get backstage?" I asked Maggie.

"I don't know," she answered, "But let's find out."

We saw the security guard standing at the door and the entrance to the backstage. We walked up to him and told him we'd like to go backstage and see Clarence Carter.

"Is he here yet?" We asked.

"I don't know," he said. "But I'll go back and check."

He went back to the room that had Clarence Carter's name on the door. He knocked on the door.

"Who's there?" Clarence asked.

Calvin and Cassandra Hightower's kids. Left to right: Jordan, Nikki, Jasmin, Callen.

Teddy Pendergrass and Candi Staton. We had many tours together.

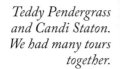

James Peeples, Maggie Staton, and my Grandbaby. My sister Maggie and brother-in-law James rescued me from the below poverty lifestyle with four children to raise alone. I'll be forever grateful. Thank You. You were a Godsend for the little girl, my granddaughter, Christina.

"Little Anthony." He used to be the lead singer for
The Imperials. I've toured with him. He is such a
wonderful person.

August 26, 1994.
Christina 18 months,
Brandon 4 years,
Janeka 8 years.

This is a younger version of
my 5 children. Front to back:
Clarence Jr., Terry, Marcel,
Cassandra, and Marcus. We're
backstage at the Kennedy
Center. Luther Vandross rode
with us just for fun

Dionne Warwick. I was on one of her "specials" in Los Angeles. I've known her so long.

1976 Young Hearts Run Free Show. Back in the day, I did quite a lot of "Chittlin Circuit" gigs. This was one of them.

Jessie Jay. What a beautiful lady. Her father told me he bought my records when she was 5 years old and said, "Listen to her and learn," and she did. I love this young lady. I pray she goes all the way.

David Gest and I met when he was married to Liza Minnelli. I've known him for about 16 years. He's been my friend.

My guitar player, Mark, and I at the BBC Record Promotions Tour, London, England. The BBC always welcomed me with open arms. Thank you BBC.

Marcus Williams family.

We were touring with David Gest, 2014. Left to Right: Candi Staton, Martha Wash, Billy Paul, Sheila Ferguson (3 Degrees), Deniece Williams, Kim Weston. We had a ball! What great entertainers.

This is Clarence Carter Jr.'s family. He is my youngest son whose dad is Clarence Carter. Left to Right: Canzetta Carter, Me, Clarence, his wife Tasha, and his youngest, Anya.

This is my son Terrence William's family. Left to Right: Terry, Brionca, Sierrea, Jenny (his wife), Landon (son).

Luther Vandross and I were friends long before he cut his first hit record. He ate lots of dinners at my house. He was such a good friend. I miss him.

Percy Sledge. The last picture I took with Percy in New York at the Premiere of the "Muscle Shoals Documentary." My daughter Cassandra and me.

Three generations of women. Me, my daughter Cassandra, and her daughter Nikki.

Just before rehearsal. What a night. Paul Shaffer was so gracious, and Dave was so amazing that night.

*My Publisher,
Sherm Smith,
and me.*

*On tour – The late Nick Ashford and Valerie Simpson, me,
and my daughter Cassandra.*

*This is the Band I've worked with for 12 years from London,
England. They are the best. Push is their name. Mark, Mic, Suzie,
Candi, Ernie, Marcus Williams (my son), Xavier.*

Cliff Richards, Freda Payne, Candi Staton,
I'm on one of Cliff's records.

I met Bobby Cox in
2010. I was at his
retirement from the
Braves in August 12,
2011. He was a fine
gentleman and always
so nice to me. I met him
through Otis Nixon.

Clarence Carter, Canzi Carter, and me
celebrating my granddaughter's birthday.

Sir Terry Wogan at BBC Radio 2. Terry was the most honored D.J. in U.K. history. May you rest in God's arms, Terry.

Nile Rodgers. Chic on tour. I can't count the shows I've done with this group on Festivals in the U.K. I love to talk to Nile Rodgers. He's a wonderful friend.

Cassandra and Calvin Hightower.

This is the actual picture of "You've Got the Love Session," Chicago, June 1986. This song went Double Platinum in the U.K. This is the day I created this song in Chicago in 1985.

Candi Staton, Clarence Carter. Club "2728" Birmingham, Alabama, 1969. The first time we met. I thank Clarence Carter for introducing me to Rick Hall. That meeting was the road that's taken me to where I am today, This is the first night we worked together. Lol!

*Mrs. Clinton and I
at the White House.
I was so delighted.
She spent quite a bit
of time with me. She
was so gracious to our
group. I wish her well.*

*My good friend, Rick Hall.
I was with Rick for 8 years
or more. What a wonderful
producer. He's one of the
world's greatest. I still work
with Rick every chance I get.
We're friends for life.*

*Candi and Gloria Gaynor. "I Will Survive". My dear friend, we
have so much history, She came to my daughter's wedding. I've spent
precious time with this wonderful, talented lady. I love you Gloria.*

My oldest son, Marcel Williams, at his oldest daughter's graduation.
Me, Marcel, Christina, Janeka (graduate), his ex-wife Costina,
Cassandra, his son Brandon, his niece Nikki, and baby Jowan.

There are 50,000 people at my stage at the Glastonbury
Festival. I was in awe. What loyal, beautiful fans that
love and appreciate my music. Mark is on guitar.

I met Lynn Whitfield. We had a wonderful time together at Ashford & Simpson's "White Party" they gave every year. She is a lovely person. It was such an honor to spend the day with her.

Donald Trump and me at Atlantic City Casino. I performed there for Mr. Trump, and he took great care of me. Gary Coleman. Guys from different groups that were also performing that night.

*You've taken me places
I never dreamed
I could go... Bill
Carpenter, Publicist.
He's been with me
and helped me for 30
years. Thanks Bill.
Where would I be
without you?*

*Nick Ashford
and Candi.*

*The great Aretha Franklin and me. I have known her all my
life, and she has had a profound impact on my music.*

"Are you Clarence Carter?" The security guard asked.

"Yes, I am."

The security guard came back and told us that Clarence was back there, but he couldn't let us go back.

"Please," I said. "We need to see him. We're friends of his. He knows us. Can you please let us go back?"

"No, I can't let you go back there. Who are you anyway?"

It was time to smile and go into the flirting mode and put on some moves.

"Look," I said. "You look cute and all that, so how about going back there for me and tell him that the little girl that sang with him in Birmingham at the 2728 Club is here."

"The 20 what?"

"The 2728 Club in Birmingham, Alabama. Tell him I'm here to see him. He told me that when he got here, I should come back and see him."

The guard went back to see Clarence, and told him what I said. "Yeah, bring her on back here," Clarence told him.

When we got to Clarence's dressing room, I had funny feelings as to whether he would really remember me.

"Hey Clarence," I said.

"Canzetta?"

"Yeah, it's me. You remember my name.

"Yeah, I remembered our name with our little singing self. Did you ever get rid of that crazy man you were married to??

"Yes, I did. I'm divorced."

"You ready to go to work?"

"Go to work?"

"Yes. I need an opening act. I'll tell you what, I gotta go on. Stay out there and don't leave until I'm finished, and when I'm finished with my show, wait on me until I get dressed. I want to talk to you."

Maggie and I told James, and he was okay with waiting around. We stayed and Clarence came on after the opening act, and he was so good. He knew how to work an audience, and I was looking at him in awe and remembered Bobble "Blue" Bland so well that night.

He walked out on stage smoking a cigarette and got choked. Maggie and I started laughing. He was trying to get his breath.

"Oh no, oh no, he didn't. He didn't just do that," I said.

It took him a while to get his breath back. That's the one thing I remember that night. After Clarence came on, he sang and the show was over. He went to get dressed. People were leaving. I forgot who started the show that night. Maybe it was Cameo, but whoever it was created a lot of excitement.

Clarence came out. He was with his valet. The valet took care of him, dressed him, and made sure he looked really sharp, and he kept his wardrobe together. Clarence said he wanted to go somewhere and eat.

"Is there somewhere quiet we can go?" He asked. "I might have a problem with the fans. Is there anywhere we can go?"

"Yes there is," James said. "We can go to our house. We'll take you to our house. We have some food there that we cooked today, and we have a lot of it. It's already ready. All we have to do is warm it up."

"Hey, that sounds good to me," Clarence said enthusiastically. "I've been eating nothing but restaurant food, and I'm tired of it. Home cooking sounds so good."

We took Clarence over to James and Maggie's home. We sat in the living room, and he talked and talked. He told us that Rick Hall was looking for a female artist because Etta James just left him, and he needed another great singer.

"Etta went to Atlantic Records," Clarence said. "You know what? I think he's gonna like you."

We sat down and ate. "I'll tell you what to do." Clarence said after we were finished. "I'm going to call Rick Hall over the weekend and ask him to meet us on Monday morning if he is up for it. I'm going to ask you to meet Rick and me in Muscle Shoals."

We took Clarence to his hotel and made sure he was safe. He called us later and said that Rick told him he was free on Monday, and what time to meet with him. We drove down to Muscle Shoals, Alabama to meet with Rick Hall.

We didn't meet Rick at Fame Studios. He had us meet him at a hotel suite. Rick was there with writers that had written songs for Aretha Franklin, and other people that he was recording. Those guys didn't expect a person like me to walk in. George Jackson and Ed Cage were there and a couple of other guys.

We went up to the suite, and there was a piano in the spacious room. Rick was sitting in a chair.

"Now Clarence," Rick Hall said. "Which one of these ladies is the singer?"

"That one. That one right there," Clarence said as he gestured towards me. "This lady standing by me."

"Clarence are you sure she can sing? She's so pretty."

I sort of laughed nervously, but I will never forget a man as famous as Mr. Hall complimenting a black woman like he did me.

"Oh God, Rick," Clarence said. "You got to hear this woman sing."

"Well let's see what she can do," Rick commented.

"Do you know *Do Right Woman?*" I asked Mr. Hall.

I sat down at the piano because I could play a little bit of the song. I started singing.

"Wait a minute." Rick said as he interrupted me. " Wait just a minute. I recorded that song on Aretha Franklin."

"You're the one who recorded that song?" I almost lost my breath. You talk about being nervous? I was really nervous. Rick Hall was a famous big time producer, and who was I? I didn't know Clarence wrote *Tell Mama* when I asked him if he knew that song. Here I am again messing up in front of Rick Hall. That's how much I knew about the music industry. Not much.

After I sang *Do Right Woman,* I told Rick that I made up a little song. I sang *To Hear You Say You're Mine.* I sang it, and my voice just came out, and Rick looked like he didn't believe what he was hearing.

"Oh my goodness," Rick said. "Get the guys over here. Get Barry and Randy. Get all the guys over here. David, get all of them here. I don't care what they're doing. Find them. Tell them to meet us at the studio. We got a session to do."

We left the hotel, got in our cars, and headed for the studio. When we got there, I looked at Fame Studios, and I was amazed because

I had seen a lot of studios in Nashville and elsewhere, but nowhere that looked like this. I couldn't help the chills running up my back. It was beyond inspiring just to think of who had been in this place making hit songs.

Rick Hall turned everything on in the studio, and everybody started showing up. George got on the piano and started playing *Old Man Sweetheart*, and I started rehearsing it with him.

I found my keys that fit my voice, and we did three songs that night. *Rather Be an Old Man's Sweetheart* sold 750,000 records when it came out, and on the flip side we recorded *For You*. We put a song in the can called *Never in Public*.

I did three or four takes on each song and by then, it was probably ten o'clock. We were finished.

"Now I can't do a thing with these records we just recorded unless I get a contract," Rick said.

"Clarence what should I do?"

"You go ahead and sign his contract. It's the same contract I signed," Clarence emphatically said. "Rick is it the same contract I signed?"

"Yeah Clarence," Rick said. "Same contract, same percentage, same everything."

"Okay," Clarence answered. "I just want to make sure this little girl gets done right."

We followed Rick up to this office, and I signed the contract. He gave me a copy of it. We left the studio and drove to Nashville. I said nothing all the way home. I was beyond speechless.

CHAPTER TWELVE

Stand By Your Man

I couldn't be happier when we arrived in Nashville after the trip to Muscle Shoals. I felt rescued because I now had a clear glimpse of my future. That trip was life changing because my future looked bleak and grim. Not now. I had more hope than I ever had in my life, and I was happy for the first time in many years. I had a job, and I had something to look forward to every day.

I had placed my kids in homes of family and friends, and they were no longer going to be a hindrance to me to get on my feet. I began to think about living on White Avenue. How in the world did I survive in Cleveland with all that danger around me and still made it out of thee in one piece.

I thought about the day when I was at work when my daughter, my baby girl, twenty-four months old had a fever, and the boys were home watching her. The oldest boy was only nine years old. I had told the boys to keep a close eye on her making sure she was okay at all times.

The boys got involved with watching TV and totally forgot about Cassandra. While the boys were not paying attention, she wandered out of the house. She was so sick that she couldn't keep moving, so she laid down and put her little head on a rock. She had a temperature of one hundred four degrees. She fell asleep. A lady that lived in the same apartment complex that we lived in spotted Cassandra laying down with her head on the rock. The kind lady picked her up and took her into her apartment and nursed her while I was at work.

When I came home and found my little girl gone, I was so upset I could hardly function. I kept asking, "Where is my little girl?" I feared the worse.

"Where is my child?" I screamed at the boys.

I knew the boys were only kids and beyond that, they were boys. They kept telling behind their tears and fear that didn't know where she was. The boys were scared out of their wits.

I was outside screaming, "Cassandra, Cassandra," and the lady who had her heard me. She came out of her apartment carrying my little girl in her arms.

"I have her," the lady said. "She has a temperature, and I have made sure she was okay until you got home."

I couldn't thank that good and kind lady enough because if we lived in this day and age, her face would have been on a milk carton. Still today, I am so thankful that I was able to work my way of that apartment complex and out of Cleveland.

I didn't realize back then that behind every dark cloud there's a silver lining. There's always light at the end of the tunnel. I look back, and I realize that people come into your life for a reason whether it is a season or a lifetime. Regardless of what you have to go through, you will go through it. It may seem way too hard, and you can't make it, but perseverance, patience, and determination will pay off.

Clarence Carter called me to come to work after a couple of weeks. He sent me a plane ticket, and I flew to Macon, Georgia to meet him. Rogers Redding, Otis Redding's brother, met me at the airport and drove me to meet Clarence. He was at the Walden's Booking Agency owned and operated by Allen and Phil Walden. They booked a lot of famous people, including Otis Redding. They would become my booking agency.

After I made my deal with the Waldens, we headed to our first show, and it was really amazing. I was so nervous because I was in unchartered territory. I knew nothing about Rhythm and Blues or how to entertain. I was as green as the Alabama grass.

I will never forget the first night I performed. I probably looked every bit the mess I was. The place was sold out, and my hair was long and naturally curly. Afros were just coming into style then. They were popular with Afro-Americans. Martin Luther King was marching, and Black Power was raising that fist to the wind and chanting "Black Power."

I was so nervous that I couldn't connect with the audience no matter how hard I tried. People in the audience started heckling me. "Whatever happened to Baby Jane," they were chanting after the Betty Davis, Joan Crawford movie of the same name.

"Don't worry we'll fix 'em," Clarence said when I ran off the stage crying.

We took off and drove all night to get to the next show. I was so angry, and all I could think was, *Why am I here? Why did this have to happen to me?* I was not in good shape.

I met Jerry Butler, and he gave me some important pointers on how to entertain. I learned from him that singing in public clubs and other venues is a whole lot different than singing in church. I can't express how much I learned from Jerry, and how much I appreciate him.

"You got to connect with the audience, Candi," Jerry said. "You can't look up at the ceiling lights, and keep looking all around you. Look at the people in the eye and sing to them. Sing to them like you were singing to the church. Look 'em in the eye and get into where they are right now in their lives. You know, just get into it, honey. Make 'em feel you.

I promised Jerry that I would work hard trying to accomplish everything he was instructing me to do. My tact may be a little unusual, but I started watching sexy movies and mimicked the moves the girls made. I cut my hair and grew an Afro. I thought I was ready.

I had no trouble rocking the house from that time forward. I had men drooling over me, and the women green with envy. I was an entertainer in the R&B Clubs. In those days you had to sing and be the real deal. The crowds back then knew who could sing, and who was a wannabe. Today, the singers get away with a lot. There isn't the talent out there now there was back then. That's why the old guard is making comebacks.

If you can't sing, there are electronic devices that put your voice in tone and on key. In the old days, you had to sing or get booed off the stage, and they would throw stuff at you. They would call you names, tell you to shut up, and everybody in there would laugh with them. There is always a guy who is the heckler leader, and the rest of the crowd jumps right in with him. It can be horrible disconcerting and embarrassing.

I had to learn to connect with the audience and hold their attention for at least an hour. That takes a lot of skill, and something you can't teach. It is a talent you have and develop from deep inside yourself that comes out during your performance and touches everybody that's listening, and you don't let him or her go until you're ready to let him or her go. It's a feeling of being real. You can't fake it. People know. It's like the calling out of the deep. When I got in that zone, I loved it. I know that's why they call it "Soul Music." "Soul" is your mind, will, and emotions. You deal with these three components when you're singing. Those are the three things I had to learn to deal with.

It was amazing how I used to reach into those audiences, and pull out something in them that they didn't even know they were feeling. Emotions would start coming out, and people would be crying. I would have some of them standing up and shouting "You better sing that song, girl." They wanted more. I had to learn how to put a show together, and how to sing every song with meaning and feeling.

I learned to entertain, and I learned the hard way. I went through trials and errors until I learned to connect with my people; and to this day, I know how to take an audience and put them in the palm of my hand and never let them go until I was ready for them to go. You know you've connected when you let them go, but they don't want to go. They want more; they aren't finished with you. They want you back up and entertaining them some more. Those are the times that you know without a doubt that you've connected with the audience.

We were making a lot of gigs, and eventually Rick Hall signed with Capital Records. I was the first Rhythm and Blues artist that they signed. Capital Records had recently opened their Rhythm and Blues section of the company. I toured seven cities with them when we got started. I sang the song *I'd Rather Be an Old Man's Sweetheart* that had just come out.

Capital Records took me to Los Angeles, and I went shopping. I was sporting my Afro hairstyle. We bought clothes that were going to make me look good. I had never seen a make-up artist before, but I found myself sitting in a salon while I was being fitted with lashes and being made beautiful. I remember thinking how much fun this career was going to be.

We made photographs during the picture session, and we got the album released. Now, the seven-city run was about to begin. We played in New Orleans and then Chicago. We played in Philadelphia, Los Angeles, New York, Atlanta, and Dallas. These were major cities where the most records would be sold.

They invited all the major artists in the city and all the mom and pop record stores. These stores included the tiny record shops on the corners that used to sell a lot of records. They had invited all the record suppliers. Warner Brothers and all their promotion people were there plus DJ's from all over the city. Everybody that was important to getting a record off the ground and putting it on the air, and selling records were in attendance at these multi-city events.

These were some kinds of events, and they were geared to sell records. They fed these people steaks, prime rib, salads, and all the Champagne they could drink. The DJ's were wined and dined and had a great time. Meanwhile, the only thing that could be heard was *I'd Rather Be an Old Man's Sweetheart.* They were masters at selling records and making songs and artists big hits.

They don't do this any more. This is not how artists are made these days. There aren't any A&R Departments that function like they used to. Today, it's all digital, and everybody's pretty much on his or her own. Back in the day, they would spend millions of dollars promoting you until you became a household name. They did quite a job with me, and I appreciate all the things these big companies did to make my singing career become what it was and is today.

The record started jumping off the shelves. I think one reason the sales were so strong was because people thought I was Aretha Franklin. It was all over the radio, and the song was written for Aretha. I just happened to be at the right place at the right time to be able to record that particular song. I don't know if it went gold or not, but we sold several hundred thousand records.

The big hit I had was *Stand by Your Man.* That was a huge song for Tammy Wynette, but I was nominated for a Grammy with Capital Records for it. This was an amazing journey I was traveling. I had my kids situated, and then Clarence and I started getting closer and closer. We would ride together after my record was released. We were riding together while the song more and more popular, and then I started getting dates on my own.

The times I was off, Clarence would always book me on his shows, so I could be close to him, and so we started dating. We were actually dating. People around back then had the same curiosity they have today. Everyone then and now was asking me why I wanted to marry a blind man. I answered then just like I answer now. "Because he couldn't see."

My ex-husband was such a stickler about me looking at people, and he was so insanely jealous, he wouldn't allow me to look out the window. I had to sit looking at him in the car while he was driving. I did look at people because everybody looks at everybody else, and now I could feel safe with a man who couldn't see where I was looking. Besides, who can help who they look at, or help who's looking at you?

I didn't have any badgering me all the time and having jealous fits of rage. I got out of harm's way by marrying a blind man. We started dating when *Stand by You Man* came out. It was a huge record for me. It was a big, big crossover. That's when I went to Las Vegas and started performing in Vegas shows, and got out of the "Chitlin Circuit" for a while. I got away from the atmosphere of people abusing me on the stage, screaming, and heckling me until I left the stage.

I stayed in Vegas for a week, and then there were other shows I did. I was on a lot of Country and Western shows because Tammy Wynette put out *Stand by Your Man* first as a pure country song, and I put out the pop version of the song.

I was on these Country and Western shows with some major artists. I did a special with Roy Clark and Sammi Smith. I was getting a lot of attention along the way. I was not only getting recognized as a Rhythm and Blues singer but also Pop music. I was selling Pop records for the first time.

I had the chance to go really big. When *Stand by Your Man* was playing, there were to men that came to Rick Hall's office at Fame Studios in Muscle Shoals, Alabama. Rick called Clarence and I to come up to his to meet him on a Saturday. The song was playing on the ABC Stations all over the world. It was rising up the charts very quickly.

These men coming to Rick's office showed up in fancy suits carrying their briefcases. They asked me if I was interested in signing with them. I'm not sure about it, but I have always believed there was a little Mafia influence involved with these guys.

They told us they would give me quite a lot of money and if I didn't ask any questions, they would make me a superstar like Diahann Carol, and everybody else that was Las Vegas material.

Clarence told them no. He flat turned them down to their surprise, and said we weren't going that way. He asked them a whole lot of questions, so they closed up their briefcases and walked out the door.

In a few weeks, *Stand By Your Man* started moving down the charts. It didn't stay up there as long as we had hoped, but that's the way the industry is. I look back, and I realized that God didn't plan for me to make that move and sign with those guys in Rick Hall's office. I probably would have signed simply out of the ecstasy of being recruited and the money. God had someone there to step in the way and make the decision for me. Clarence saved me from signing a blind contract and perhaps being messed up the rest of my life.

Clarence and I got closer and closer, and while *Stand By Your Man* was going all the way off the charts, I realized I was pregnant. I was pregnant with my son, Clarence Carter, Jr.

"Clarence, I can't afford to have this child," I told him. "I coming down off the charts, and I already have four children. I don't know what I'm going to do. I don't want...I do not want...I won't get an abortion, but I don't know what to do."

I didn't know what I was thinking, but I was upset.

"Clarence, I can't have this baby," I said to Clarence.

"What in the world are you trying to tell me?" He said. "Are you trying to run away? What are you trying to say?"

"I don't know. I just..."

"Look, that's my baby too, and we're going to get married."

"We are?" I reacted in pure amazement at what he just said.

"Yeah, we are, we're going to get married."

We made our plans, and we got married. I was about four months pregnant when we tied the knot. *Wow, here I go again.* I was four months pregnant when I walked down the aisle and got my high school diploma, and now four months pregnant when I walked down the aisle to get married. *Lord, I have a way of repeating history,* I said to him.

When Clarence and I got married three of my kids were living with her. I bought a trailer house and parked it next to my mother's house. Marcus was the only child that didn't come home with us because Betty, who took Marcus when I needed help, didn't want to give him back. Eventually, I found a way to persuade her to let him go, and he came to live with us.

We had a beautiful trailer out there, and we had the best of both worlds. We had mama's cooking, and we had our own home. We were all together. Cassandra was seven years old. I had been on the road with Clarence for three years, and then I went on my own for a while, and then here comes the baby. We moved to Montgomery, Alabama.

Clarence and I took the trailer back to the dealer, and they took it back with no questions. They had not problem getting all their money out of it in a real quick sale because this was Clarence Carter and Candi Staton, and people wanted to own a home that we had owned.

We moved into Clarence's home in Montgomery. We had lots of room for the kids. We added on a new spacious den that made the house even larger. I had the baby. My boy was born in Montgomery, and I remember so well the day he was born. Clarence was in Antiqua Bay with his band. I called him and told him I was in labor.

"I'll be home, I'll be home, soon," he said.

Clarence arrived back in Montgomery after the baby had come. I was home from the hospital when Clarence walked in. He goes straight to the baby and picks him up.

"You're gonna name this baby Clarence George Carter, Jr.," he determined.

"Well okay then, that's the boy's name," I said.

"I don't have any other kids, but I'll have a Junior."

"Well, Sir, you got one now."

I immediately started recuperating from childbirth, and I was trying to lose some weight and get back on the road.

I was going through Clarence's briefcase one day looking for some cash, and I found an airline ticket. The ticket was for a trip to Antiqua Bay, and it was made to Mr. and Mrs. Clarence Carter, Sr. I knew that couldn't be me because I was having a baby. I wondered who in the world were Mr. and Mrs. Clarence Carter?

"Clarence, what is this?" I read to him what was on the ticket.

"Oh," he replied. "They made a mistake over at the travel agency." He explained.

"How could they make that kind of mistake, Clarence? Were you in Antiqua with another woman?"

Well, you know we don't have a girl that's opening for me, and no, I ain't, I mean that's the only woman."

"Are y'all dating? Are y'all fooling around?

Clarence got real defensive, and he got very mad, so he started raising his voice, and I was thinking *Yeah, they are fooling around.* I kept going on and on with it, and I knew he was cheating on me.

I began putting out my own reviews, and I got all the components together for my own band. I hired the musicians, and I bought a bus. I had everything I needed to get my own gigs.

"Clarence, you and I could have the greatest show. I could open for you, and all the money would be coming into the same household. "

"No, you do your thing, and I will do my thing."

Clarence wouldn't hear of it, and I was sure he other things on his mind to occupy his time. Things got worse, and he was cheating more and more. I could see from the telltale signs when he got home what he was doing. I don't have to tell all the details, but I knew for a fact he was cheating. Like the song, *Lipstick on Your Collar,* and the smell of perfume I never used, hotel matches in his pocket, and a strange door key, and guilt all over his face was all the evidence I needed.

I was not going to put up with him. Those were the kinds of things I wouldn't tolerate in my marriage, so I started making my own money. We came to an agreement and decided to stay together and try to make it as husband and wife. We really did try.

During the time we were trying to fix our marriage, my brother was driving for us. He had recently come home from Vietnam. He got a job with UPS and moved to Alexandria, Virginia and Skeet, his brother, came home from college at Memphis State University and moved in with us. Skeet and Clarence became close. He was watching me and made his move.

"Let me tell you now," Clarence declared. "We're never going to have anyone living in our house. We're just not going to do it. That means your family or my family."

I told him that was perfectly fine with me. Robert couldn't live with us but when Skeet came, he moved in with us.

"You told me that there would be nobody living with us," I reminded him. When Skeet came, Clarence spent more time with him than he did with me. They went to all kinds of places together including lunch all the time. I was at home by myself most of the time while they were running around. Skeet drove Clarence everywhere, and he would make arrangements for Clarence. He was right by his side.

My publisher, Sherm Smith, who helped write this book, told me while we were dealing with this story, "Something that fails in the end had a fatal fall in the beginning."

When I first started dating Clarence, I was aware that new relationships always have some loose ends that have to be tied up with another woman involved. I had no idea that Clarence had a girlfriend. I went with him to Montgomery one time during a tour, and I met this lady.

The lady's name was Shirley, and she was working at the record shop Clarence owned. She looked at me like she could run over me with a truck. Her eyes were full of hatred and if looks could kill, I wouldn't be around today.

"Clarence, what's going on between you and Shirley?" I said as I confronted the situation.

"Ain't nothing going on between Shirley and me," he said. "She's over my business right now, and she takes care of my checking and the money. That's what she does."

"Really? That's all that's going on between you guys?"

"Oh, yeah, yeah, yeah. I mean, you know, we got a little girl now. We got a baby together."

"Do you? You have a daughter by her? Y'all have been dating. I think maybe y'all may still be dating. Tell me the truth. I want to know the truth."

Well, we, you know, you know how things are. I'm going to straighten it out. Give me time to straighten this out."

"Clarence, please don't' put me in jeopardy. I'll move out of the way while you straighten this out."

"No. Don't do that. I'll take care of it."

We were in St. Louis, and Clarence and I used to get adjoining rooms, and so sometimes we would end up in the same room. This particular morning we had arrived before we were to do a show that night. There was a phone call and when he answered, somebody hung up. The person called right back and when he answered, the person hung up again.

"Huh, that's strange," I said.

We got dressed and had lunch, and then got ready for the show.

About twenty minutes after we got there, lo and behold in walks Shirley into our dressing room with two other girls with her. I didn't feel good at all about this. I was in there getting dressed for the show because I always helped him to get dressed. We used the same dressing room. I made sure all his clothes matched, and he had on the right shoes.

I went out and did my show, and Clarence was in the dressing room ready to go out and do his show. I went in the dressing room, and Shirley was still in there with those other two women. Clarence walked out. He never told me to leave and go hang with Roger, wait somewhere else. He left me in the dressing room with those women.

We did two shows a night, and I had just walked off the stage all sweaty and ready to change into my casual clothes and relax for a while.

"We came here for nothing else but to beat your ass," Shirley said.

"What? What have I done to you?" I answered.

"You think you gonna take my man, bitch? You have another thought coming," Shirley said nastily.

Shirley walked over to me and pushed me. She didn't only push me, she pushed me very hard. She shoved me up against the wall, so I pushed her back.

"What are you doing?" I shouted. "Stop it!"

I glanced over quickly to see where the other two girls were. I heard the sound of two switchblade knives pop out. If you've been around some bad neighborhoods, you can't miss the "click, click" sound of a switchblade opening up.

"If you touch her, put your hands on her, we're gonna cut you in little pieces" one of the rough girls said.

Oh, my God, how in the world am I going to get out of this? I was thinking. Shirley jumped me and was hitting me everywhere you could think. She knocked me on the floor, and I couldn't get up. She stepped all over my clothes, and then started kicking me. She kicked me in the head and all over my body until I was the verge of blacking out.

I could feel the room getting darker and darker, and I could hear a buzzing in my ears, and felt like I was going to pass out.

"Shirley, Shirley, that's enough. That's enough, now," I could hear one of the women yelling at her. "You ain't killing this girl. We didn't come here to be no accessory to murder. You come on, let's go, let's go. You've done enough, let's go."

I was out cold and when I came to, and I was too dizzy to stand up. I worked my way to the door and pulled myself up. I was wobbling all over the place barely standing, and then I thought maybe I had a concussion and very seriously injured. I could still see those fishnet stockings landing blows to my body. I can't forget those huge feet she had, and the fishnet stockings on her feet.

Shirley was trying her best to destroy my face. She busted my lip, and I had blood running out of my head. I had no idea how badly I was hurt. I had sat back down on the floor, but eventually had the strength to pull myself up on the doorknob. Roger was seated outside on a stool watching the show.

"Roger," I faintly called to him. "Roger."

"Oh, my God, what in the world?" He said when he came in the room. "Oh, Lord, I knew I should've come in here. I knew Clarence shouldn't have left you with those women."

He carried me to the sink and ran water over my head as blood was pouring out. He held the wound with his hands stopping the blood flow enough until it finally stopped bleeding. My lip was a mess – swollen and bleeding. My face was badly bruised, and I was bruised all over my body.

"Do you want to go to the hospital?" Roger asked.

"Yes, I definitely need to go," I answered. "Take me to the emergency room."

"Or you okay long enough for me to get Clarence off the stage?" Roger asked.

I took a couple aspirin with some water that Roger gave to me to help ease the pain. He sat down with my head in his lap and held me comforting me until it was time to go get Clarence. He always walked Clarence off the stage. While they were walking back to the dressing room, Roger was telling Clarence that Shirley had beat me up pretty badly.

Clarence let the band go on back to the hotel, so they wouldn't see me, and then the three of us headed for the hospital. The doctor who examined me had x-rays taken, and determined that I didn't have a concussion. He said there was minor bruising that would go away without any permanent damage, but he wanted me to be sure that no blood veins popped up or burst. There were no weak blood vessels. They wanted to stitch my lip, but I wouldn't let them. I was going to hold to closed until it healed, and I wouldn't have a deformed lip. The doctor asked me if I wanted him to call the police, and did I want to press charges.

"Don't call the police," Clarence said after I asked him what he wanted to do. "I'm gonna handle this. I'm handling this."

We did our next show, and I didn't feel like doing two of them. I couldn't go on. At the next town, we stayed there. We took off an entire week and stayed in the hotel. Clarence wanted me to take the time off and make sure I was fully recuperated from the ordeal.

Clarence went home to Montgomery and had Shirley indicted because she had also taken all his money. She fraudulently took his money from his bank account. She took off, but the cops found her, arrested her, and she was indicted. They sentenced Shirley, and she went to prison. Clarence did take care of what he promised he would.

Clarence and I continued to date, finally got married, had the baby and moved to Montgomery. When Clarence, Jr. was six weeks old, I went back on the road, and the cheating had started. Skeet came out of college, and everything changed.

When I was in bed at night, I could hear Clarence and Skeet talking. *You know what to do,* were my thoughts. *You know how the women out there are chasing and looking.* It was horrible. By then, I could take care of myself thanks to Clarence. He did provide me with that area where I could be self sufficient, and he introduced me to the world. I will forever be grateful to him for doing what he did for me, but the other part of our lives, I simply couldn't take it.

The kids loved Clarence. We had been together for about three years, and there was cheating. He was constantly cheating and wasn't going to quit. I finally decided it time for me to start going out.

There was a song called *Mr. and Mrs. Untrue,* and I had sung that song one night, and we headed for home. We were listening to the song on the radio. I was getting ready to go on the road, and I didn't want to go out there by myself. There is so much temptation that is so strong. I didn't want to go without my own husband with me. I was trying to get next to Clarence, but he pushed me away. I will never forget what happened that night.

"You know that song you just did?" Clarence asked.

"Which one?"

"The last one you…"

"Are you talking about *Mr. and Mrs. Untrue?*"

"Yeah, that one," he said. "Why don't you go try that one? Why don't' you do that. Why don't you just do what that song says?"

"Are you telling me to cheat on you?"

I sort of laughed at his comments. I didn't cheat on him, and I wouldn't. I never tried anything because I'm not that kind of person. I don't believe in cheating. Things got worse and worse. Skeet was in our home, and started watching me and telling Clarence that I was going out on him. Skeet would touch the car hood to see if it was warm I hadn't been anywhere. He was Clarence's watchdog.

Clarence was dating this girl on the road. Her name was Katie. I found out about it, and I told him I was leaving him, and I did. Katie came to the house one night, and I confronted both of them. I made her leave the house immediately, and that got him good.

I told him that I wasn't handling his cheating with this woman, and I left the house. I stayed out awhile and then returned. Clarence told me he wasn't getting rid of Katie, so I told him he would be getting rid of one of us.

"One of us has to go," I told him.

"I'm keeping Katie," he said.

I went out on a Wednesday night. It was Ladies Night, so I went with my friend, Margie. When I came home, it was around eleven or twelve o'clock. Skeet and Clarence hadn't come in yet. When they did come home, Skeet asked me where I'd been.

"I am not your wife," I told him. Don't you ever ask me where I've been. Do you understand little boy? You're going to get out of my business and stay out of my business."

"So where were you last night?" Clarence asked me the next morning.

"I went out with Margie. We went to Ladies night at the club. On Wednesday nights they have Ladies night at this club in Atlanta."

"Well," he began. "I'm gonna tell you right now that I'm gonna make some rules around this place."

"Rules? Does that go for you, too?"

"I'm making some rules for you," he explained. "You better be in this house by twelve o'clock midnight. No later than eleven thirty or twelve o'clock, and you don't stay out no later. You better make sure everything is done around here. You make sure you ain't running around with Margie. You're gonna make sure…"

"You are dreaming," I said. "Who the hell do you think you're talking to? I am not sixteen years old. I'm not your daughter, so you don't make a curfew. Do you understand? Meanwhile, you are out screwing every woman you can, and you're gonna tell me to be home at eleven o'clock? You can kiss my ass."

Clarence didn't say anything. He wouldn't say anything. The baby was two years old, and Junior was crying. We were arguing, and the boy was crying. We had this long table in the kitchen. Clarence was like all blind people. He would go around the table rubbing the side, so he could measure the distance to the stove.

In those days, we had percolators to make coffee. The coffee was on the stove. Clarence makes his way to the stove and grabs his coffee cup. He made a pretense that he was going to refill his cup.

Clarence got to where I was standing, he grabbed me. Of course this was totally unexpected, and he got the upper hand on me. He held tightly to my clothes, and then started beating me in the face. He was shaking me violently with all his strength. He slams me, and throws me down. I am trying to get away from him, but he is strong. I am fighting with him, and we finally lose our balance and hit the floor.

Clarence straddled me. He got his body over me, and started beating me in the face and on my chest. He kept it up and wasn't going to stop.

"Clarence, you're hurting me," I screamed. "Stop it, stop it. Don't do this to me. You're hurting me, you're hurting me. Get off me."

Clarence wouldn't quit hitting me. I did the only thing I could think to do. I collapsed and went limp like I was dead. He stopped hitting me. I pretended that I wasn't breathing. I was holding my breath, and he was trying to feel my nose and see if I was breathing.

I had taken a very deep breath, so he couldn't feel any air coming from my nose or mouth. Clarence thought he killed me. He got up from the floor and went into the bedroom. He was calling out my name, but I wouldn't answer. Our floors were carpeted, so I got up quietly and went into the bedroom. I tiptoed into the bedroom closet. I had a loaded gun in there. It was a 32 caliber. I grabbed the gun, and the Devil told me to kill him. The Devil told me to blow him away.

I pointed the gun at him. He's blind, so he couldn't see me pointing the gun at his head. I then heard the voice of wisdom say.

You will be in jail the rest of your life, the voice said. *Can you believe you would kill Clarence Carter? He can't see. You would have killed a blind man. You'll get over your wounds, but you won't get over this. Your career will be over, and what's going to happen to your kids?*

I froze in place, and then I went back to the closet and put the gun away. I went into the bathroom and got dressed. I went into another bedroom of the house, and I called my friend, Leroy Hadley, who was my bandleader at that time.

"Leroy," I said on the phone. "Clarence has jumped me. He beat me up real bad."

We had a show coming up that weekend, and this was Thursday. There was no urgency in Leroy's voice, and he started laughing.

"What are you laughing about Leroy," I asked him. "This ain't no joke. This ain't funny."

"Candi, how does a blind man beat you up?"

"I'll let you know when I get there. I am dizzy, so I hope I can drive."

I got dressed and put on a lot of makeup, and I put on a pair of sunglasses. I had met an attorney by the name of Don Weissman at a club one night. He told me if I ever needed him to contact him. He had recently finished law school and became a great attorney in the Atlanta area. I remembered where I put his card, and I called him.

"Come down here right now," Mr. Weissman said. "I want to take photos."

I arrived at Leroy's apartment. He used to call me Pete.

"Pete, good Lord," he said when he saw me. "He tried to kill you, didn't he?"

"He wanted to kill me, but he didn't. I'm a tough cookie."

Leroy drove the baby and I to downtown Atlanta, and we went to Don Weissman's office. Don already had a photographer ready to take photos. He took a lot of photos, and they were vibrant. My eyes were blackened, and my face and neck was badly bruised, and my lip was busted. You could easily see where he had choked me. I was hurt badly.

Leroy and I left Don's office, and we were ready to go back to Leroy's apartment.

"I have to go home," I told Leroy.

"Pete, if I were you I wouldn't go home."

Don knew where there were some suites you could move into without furnishing. He made a call and then called me and told me he had found a suite he wanted me to move into.

I made sure Clarence wasn't home, and I went over there and got some clothes for the kids and me. We moved into the suite and stayed there. I filed for divorce.

CHAPTER THIRTEEN
I Guess You Don't Love Me No More

I was leaving my house and getting away from the abuse, and I want to leave a message right here to men and women. You can control your anger. In the midst of all that happened in my marriage to Clarence Carter, it would have been easy to pull the trigger of the gun in my hand and kill him. I had a choice, and I had to think through that choice in seconds.

My mother always taught me to think before I acted, and that such great advice. I'm glad she taught me that before I do something I may be sorry for later, think about the consequences first. There are so many men and women in jail today for killing their spouses. They didn't have to do that. They could have moved on and spared a life and themselves the heartaches of a life in prison.

Many people have asked me why I've had so many husbands; why have I divorced so many men? You're going to read in this book all those reasons I had to leave those men. It's not so bad when you can call two men and a truck on any given day and get away from a situation that you think is going to ruin your life.

I was determined not to ruin my life on foolishness. I could also find another man. I don't have to sit in jail for thirty year or more for something that I did in a split second that will control my life for the rest of my life. No way was I about to do that. I wasn't going to allow any man to do that to me. I am not going to give to another person that kind of authority over me, or their will over mine, and force me to do something that I will regret for the rest of my life.

How long would I have to sit in jail thinking about what I'd done, and how I could have avoided it. No, I fought emotions under control before I committed the crime. If I can control it, you can control it.

Leroy and I left Don Weissman's office and were on the way out of Atlanta. We were stuck in a very slow moving traffic jam. Out of nowhere, this homeless guy jumps on the hood of our car and tells us to run over him.

"I want you to run over me and kill me," he said.

"Man, get off the car," Leroy yelled at the man because he wouldn't let go.

"No, I don't want to live today," he cried. "I want to die. Run over me, run over me."

"Dear God," I said out loud. "Now Lord, this makes no sense. I had the opportunity to kill Clarence today, and this guy wants me to finish the job by killing him?"

The guy finally got off the car, and we sat still for a minute, and then burst we burst out laughing. As sad as the time was, we couldn't help it.

We lived in the Homeland Suites until the divorce was final. I had my kids, but I was depressed. No one will know but God how depressed I was. I was losing my husband, my family, and I felt like I was losing everything.

I thought I would be with Clarence forever because we worked so well together. We accomplished a lot. I couldn't live in the atmosphere that finally worked it way into our lives.

Clarence and I filed our taxes jointly before the marriage blew up. I had opened a Post Office box to receive my mail rather than have it delivered to the apartment. One morning I went to the Post Office box to pick up my mail. In the box was a Registered Mail notice announcing that I needed to pick up a delivery.

I picked up the mail, and there was a letter from the Internal Revenue Service accusing me of not paying my taxes. Clarence had my receipts divided, and he filed taxes on his own, and he had all my information destroyed.

This was one of the most hurtful things that I had to deal with during either of my marriages. I couldn't cope with the idea that I had a child with this man, and he does this to me.

I had a meeting with the IRS, and they told me that I owed ten thousand dollars in back taxes. Clarence said I had been paying my and taking out the taxes but not paying the withholding taxes. He told them many things that would get me into trouble.

"Mom, can you come down and pick up the kids for me?" I asked when I called her. "Clarence and I are getting ready to divorce, and I'm not home. I'm in this little apartment."

"Yeah, we'll come down," she said.

Mr. Marsh and my mother came to Atlanta and found the little suite where we were living. They took all the children to Alabama, so they would have a place to play during the summertime.

I was in a depressed state, and I had never been so depressed in my life. I understand people who are depressed and what they are going through. Even so, I had plans.

I kissed all my children goodbye when they were ready to leave with my mom. I kissed her, and I hugged Mr. Marsh. I cried as I watched the kids leave for Alabama.

The day before the kids left, I had gone to the doctor. I told him I was having difficulty sleeping, and I explained to him what I was going through. He prescribed sleeping pills. I had made plans to end my life. I was going to take an overdose of pills and sleep my life away. I would let my mother finish raising my kids, and let the IRS get the money from wherever they could.

I didn't care anymore. I was done. I had been through hell with

Joe and through hell with Clarence. I'm in my second marriage, and I have five kids. I was at the end of my rope, and I felt like I couldn't live another day on this earth. I was as bad as the homeless guy. I wanted to die today.

I pondered after the kids were gone how the suicide would be. I wouldn't know anything. I would take the pills, lie down, go to sleep, and wake up somewhere out there.

I went in the bathroom and ingested twenty-four sleeping pills and lay down on my pillow to die. I soon felt the effects of the pills starting to work. I began to feel drowsy, and all of my children flashed through my mind. I know this had to be Divine intervention because I saw each of my kids as plain as day, and they were all smiling.

All of a sudden, I had this overwhelming desire that I did not want to die. *What am I doing? I don't want to die.*

"Oh God," I prayed. "If you're so real, and you don't' want me to die. If you're real, stop me; stop me right now. I don't know how you're going to do it, Lord, but do something to help me."

I sat up and had the strength to drink some water. When I drank, I felt real sick to my stomach. My stomach turned upside down, and I ran to the bathroom, and I threw up every pill I swallowed. I counted the pills. They were floating in the toilet. I felt only a little sleepy because the pills hadn't dissolved.

I started weeping. I began crying and crying.

"Lord please, help me. Help me God. I don't know what to do. Please help me." I pleaded with the Savior.

I called Roger Redding. He was my friend.

"Roger, guess what I just did? I took twenty-four sleeping pills."

"What?" He said. "I'll be there as fast as I can."

Roger must have driven one hundred miles an hour because it seemed like no time, and he was banging on my door. He stayed the whole night to make sure I was going to be stable and not try to hurt myself again.

"I'm all right, Roger," I told him. "You didn't let me finish my conversation with you before you hung up and took off. I was going to tell you the pills didn't work because I vomited all of them into the toilet."

We talked a long time, and I told him how badly I felt, and that's why he decided to stay the night.

"I'm going to stay here because I don't want you doing anything else that crazy." He warmly said.

"Oh, you don't need to worry about that any more. I will never do try that again."

I had to deal with the divorce. It came time for us to go before the Judge, and he tried to work out some deals with Clarence, but they weren't going to work. The Attorney's were talking.

Don Weissman was a tough guy. He was talking to Clarence's Attorney when we got into the courtroom that morning. I will never forget how he briefed me.

"Now, we're going before this Judge, and this Judge hates men that beat up women. You have to know that Clarence will always get sympathy because of his handicap. That won't matter to this Judge."

We were in the courtroom. Clarence was on one side, and I was on the other. The Judge called our case.

Clarence's Attorney got up to state his side of the case. He said I was a liar and went on and on about my lack of credibility because of lying.

Don stood up and showed the Judge photos of how badly I had been beaten by this blind man. That was all the Judge needed.

"This doesn't need to go any farther," the Judge stated. "I've seen all I need to know."

I was crying when they put me on the stand. I told them how he beat me, and how he was a cheater. I told the Court everything.

The Judge awarded me everything I wanted.

"I give you an extra twenty-five thousand dollars because he put his hands on you," the Judge said proudly.

Don was kicking my foot under the table. He was letting me know that this Judge really didn't have any sympathy on a man that beats up a woman whether he can see or not.

The Judge gave me a lot of money and four hundred dollars a month on behalf of Clarence, Jr. for child support.

On our way out of the courtroom, Don and Clarence's Lawyer almost went to blows. They were yelling at each other, and the Bailiff came out and broke it up before they started slugging at each other.

"You pulled that trick on me," Clarence's Attorney shouted. "I didn't know you had photos. You made me look like a fool in there."

The divorce was final, and I got everything I wanted and needed to make ends meet. It was fair, and I was happy.

Don helped me buy a house. I had bought it before the divorce was final having moved out of the apartment. I wanted my kids, so I bought the house. The kids had a new school named Sandtown Elementary. I look at my children now, and I want to say this about them.

My kids are troopers. Most kids that had been moved around as much as my kids were would be into nothing but trouble. I uprooted my kids so many times it was pitiful. Every time they started getting remotely settled, I moved them to some other place. We moved from city to city. I was doing something different and running around with somebody else.

As I look at them today, they turned out to be excellent people. They are first class citizens, successful, and hard working individuals. They've made good homes. If I had it to do all over again, I would not have moved those kids around like I did and put them through the hell they had to endure.

I am sorry about uprooting them here and there, moving out of this house and into another house, a man moving into the house, and then a different guy they had to put up with.

I made the record, *Life Happens,* and I can't change what has been or what is.

I moved into another phase of my life. I went on the road again. My kids are in a beautiful home on two acres of land, they're in a new school, and I got a wonderful Nanny to watch over them. Things were good. They really, really were good.

THE CHITLIN CIRCUIT

A circuit is like a certain class or a clique. There are many clubs and promoters in the particular circuit. I never knew much about what they were referring to when I entered the R&B music in 1969. I was so green because I never did anything except church music, and now I'm going into another place in my life that I was not familiar with.

I kept hearing that expression over and over again. There are a lot of promoters in the Chitlin Circuit. They would say things like, "We can keep Candi pretty busy."

The Walden Agency was who booked us. The Agency was a father and two sons that managed the clientele. Phil Walden and Allen Walden ran the business. Allen and Phil are the ones who discovered the Allman Brothers. The Walden's booked everybody who was anybody, and you didn't have to sign with them to get booked.

If a gig came open, they would call you and ask if you could do it. If you agreed, they would give you a contract for that particular event. They kept fifteen percent of the gross amount. They controlled everything going on in the Chitlin Circuit. Some things were horrible in there, and some things were good.

It was an amazing experience, and it's how I learned to perform and run a show. I got so much experience on the Circuit; it was like going to college after you have sung in so many churches, and now you are introduced to a whole new world.

I was so green. I didn't know anything. I had my share of being booed off the stage by a hostile audience, and I had no idea how to handle those situations. I felt so rejected and depressed. I had been singing in churches were the crowd was appreciated, and where there was no violence coming from the congregation. They would embrace you and tell you how wonderful you are and love on you. Now, I was in a whole new genre I knew nothing about and had to face hostilities toward singers and music I never knew existed.

I knew how to sing, but I knew nothing about entertaining. Once an artist learns what to do on stage in this circuit, he or she can hold their own with the best of them. In my opinion, Soul music was born in the Chitlin Circuit. People were entertained in "Juke Joints." There was no band, so the jukebox was the source of music the entertainers on the circuit used.

"Blue Lights in the Basement" was another place people were entertained in places far from cities where there were no stages or venues for normal performances. The people formed a little club, and they would meet at somebody's house and put blue lights in the basement. They would bring their booze and get entertained by someone on the Chitlin Circuit.

If wanted real "soul music," you didn't go to concerts because it didn't exist there. You went to the Chitlin Circuit to find that kind of music that reached the inner depths of the soul.

Soul music is more than a beat, or music about money, cars, or houses. The soul singers reach down inside a person where the pain and hurt is. They reach down and found the happiness of a person who just fell in love. There were a lot of slow songs out at that time that reached the person. When you heard those songs, you cried, laughed, or danced. You did something because the music was so effective in dealing with pain, hurt, and rejections, or you told the person you were in love with to listen to a song like *Turn off the Lights* by Teddy Pendergrass. Songs like that moved you.

Songs like *Who's Been Making Love to Your Old*

Lady by Johnny Taylor would have a profound effect on those guys attending a performance. They would hear a song like this, and the lines at the pay phones would be long because the guys were out there calling home to see if anybody was cheating with their old lady. I used to open for Johnny Taylor, so I've seen these reactions and got a kick of how people would be influenced the songs of soul.

The disc jockeys used to play my song; *I'm Just a Prisoner.* Music and lyrics were so wonderful together. I think the reason we have so many oldie radio programs is because we're trying to capture what we lost. *I've Never Loved a Man, Do Right Woman,* and *Respect* were just a few of the songs back in the day that uplifted us and told us how to live.

The Civil Rights Movement brought a plethora of songs that touched the heart of the movement. What people call "Soul Music" today is nowhere near the quality of the songs back in the days of the Chitlin Circuit. I have worked with the best of them, so trust me when I tell you that the music today doesn't touch the soul like it did back then.

When I got in front of a microphone and began to sing, it was like therapy. Whatever happened to me that day good and bad, I let it go in the songs I was singing, and the audience connected and felt it, too. Soul music comes from the atmosphere you're around everyday with your family, friends, or your job. Music has changed so much because people have changed. Technology has taken over. The soulful sound of music has been replaced by the social networks and Reality shows.

You don't have to sing good anymore. The singing is phony. They can push little buttons that make you sound better than you really are. The good music is phasing out and fading away.

If the singers today were on the Chitlin Circuit, they would be booed offstage. The fans attending the Chitlin Circuits know they're stuff, so the singers had to know how to sing or pay the price. I am today who I am because I learned how to stay on the stage through an entire performance and not get run off by hostile crowd that didn't like my music. I'm still performing today because of what I learned back then.

If the Chitlin Circuit approved you, you knew you had arrived. You were ready to grace any stage in the world. Music shows on television have taken music in a new direction. We didn't have TV back then. Sam Cooke was hardly ever seen on television. If you wanted to see him, you had to catch him when he came to town. You have to experience Soul Music.

For music to be real soul, the lyrics and the music have to mesh together like two lovers. I learned how to make a song effective from my Producer, Rick Hall. Rick would make you stand there and sing until you felt that song in your soul, and it came out on the record. He wouldn't let you go until you had accomplished what he was looking for. I would get so tired that I didn't care what Rick was looking for in a song, but he wouldn't budge until he knew it was a hit.

Making a great soul song is like building a great sermon for church. The sermon has to be worked and worked, and then the preacher thunders it from the pulpit and moves the crowd. Being a great soul singer is the same thing. You have to work at getting it right, so the people hearing it will get the message. That's what Soul Music is all about.

If I really want to get into a song, I think about something evil one of exes said to me beat me up, or I go deep into my soul, and I sing until I've captured the soul of the song I'm looking for. I can't stress enough that Soul Music came from the mind and the will.

I was doing a promotion in New York working at a radio station. A young lady that worked there came running down the stairs.

"Ms. Candi, I heard you are in the building, and I just have to meet you," she exclaimed. "You don't know this, but you changed my direction when I was in school. My friends were dropping out and getting pregnant and involved in everything but what they were supposed to be doing. My mother bought your record, Young Hearts Run Free and made me listen to it every day. As a result, I graduated, went on to college and got my degree, and then landed a good job. Thank you so much for your input into my life."

I'm not sure if everybody reading this book has ever heard of the Chitlin Circuit. It was part of Ray Charles' movie *Ray*. I have a first hand experience being part of the Circuit. I guess I worked every club on the east side of the Mississippi River.

For ten years, night after night after night, I was singing in a club on the Chitlin Circuit. I wish everyone who sang on the Circuit could sit around and tell their stories and how they got started. It is a community in itself. Unfortunately, so many whose careers were born on the Circuit are no longer around, and I wanted to let you know what went on and do my part to make sure the Chitlin Circuit was always and important part of music history.

The first and the fifteenth of the month was when people had money. Welfare checks came in, payday happened, so people that had worked so hard all week would dress to the nines and head for the club were their favorite artists were performing. They looked forward to Friday and Saturday nights.

The atmosphere inside the clubs was festive. Everybody was so dressed up. Men dressed in their blue suits with open coats and shirts and jewelry hanging on their necks. The women would be wearing their finest dresses, and everybody was showing off to everybody else. The entertainers dressed with class not like they do today. I am talking about back woods clubs where people enjoyed dressing up, so the entertainers couldn't look like they just came from Walmart. We looked like stars because that is what the people expected from us. I can't imagine coming on stage with holes in my jeans and a tee shirt hanging out and trying to get inside somebody's soul. I still don't go on stage looking any kind of way. I want to impress and perform my songs.

All the people knew each other, and this was their meeting place. Instead of communion at church, they would bring their own bottle and drink. Some would get drunk, and there always was a fight or two going on until it was broken up.

Some of the promoters were dishonest. Some paid you, and some didn't. We learned as young artist to carry a gun. I became a young gangster early in my career. I bought a Smith and Wesson .32 caliber pistol and got a permit to carry it. Johnny Taylor, my very close friend, taught me what to do. He told me I would need a gun so get one.

I would walk into the office of the crooked promoter, take my gun out, and demand payment. I am sure I looked really funny to those guys, and my threats probably weren't taken seriously, but I got paid anyway.

I started working with Rick Hall, and we were marketing the songs I recorded to R&B radio stations. There were all kinds of genres of music and charts of the top songs in each one. We stayed in our genre of music because it was so hard to break out when you were known for one type of music.

The 1970's came and things got really rough. A

whole new genre of music was breaking into the world, and I was stuck where I was with the R&B and things got really rough. We didn't fit the format, so they kept us in R&B. We needed crossover potential, so that we could get our records played. At that time, the only way to get our records on the air was to slip something under the table. We called it "giving them something, something."

Crossovers are the reason you still hear songs by the Supremes and other great R&B singers. My records started crossing over when *Stand By Your Man* was released. I was Grammy nominated which greatly broadened my listening audience and record sales. My records stayed on the pop charts for a while, and then they cooled off. I was right back in the Chiltlin Circuit because R&B was my staple music, and I could always work.

To make it all work, you would bring songs that were popular in your earlier career on the Chilin Circuit, and songs that were hits while you were off the Chitlin Circuit. Al Green was a crossover act. I opened for him many, many times. I was on the road with him and knew him quite well. What a singer he was and still is. I would go on stage with him and get introduced to a lot of his fans.

Not all singers crossed over, and there are hundreds of singers still working the Chitlin Circuit all over the country. My band and I traveled every day heading to the next show. We endured all kinds of weather but kept going. We were tired of long hours of driving, and the breakdowns now and then on the bus. We would blow out a tire and be stuck.

We had trouble finding rooms because we were Afro-Americans, and that only exasperated our heavy burdens. We would finally get the clubs, and it would be half full. The club owner would be upset because we didn't draw the crowd like we were slated to. We would have to battle and argue telling him that he didn't do his job. He didn't advertise correctly and dropped the ball. Sometimes they put out one hundred placards or bought enough airtime to fill up a club.

Another thing that would kill the crowd is a bigger name playing on the other side of town. The club owner didn't do his research, which was bad for the club and us. None of us made the money we anticipated, so the Chitlin Circuit road was not an easy path.

The clubs sit so far back in the woods that most of the time, you don't even know they're there. You pass cows, horses, chickens, pigs, and open fields of crops growing. When you got out there in the woods, there would be over two thousand people waiting for you.

There were no dressing rooms, so I learned to change into my gown on the bus without revealing a thing to the guys. Don't be fooled. They were all looking and waiting from something they hadn't seen before. I always had one of them zip me up, and all of them would ogle me hoping that zipper didn't make it.

All of our dates were not Chitlin Circuit gigs. We also did concerts with many other artists. David Ruffin was my favorite, and we did many concerts together. I loved him as one of my best friends I ever had in the business. Those concerts were a real relief from the every day grind of the Chitlin Circuit.

I had a show at a club in the back woods of North Carolina. The promoter was the Mayor, the Chief of Police, and was on the City Counsel. He had made a makeshift club that was actually under a tent. He spread linoleum on the ground, so we wouldn't have to walk on the dirt.

He called me to come and sing that night. I only

had a couple records out at the time - *Old Man Sweetheart, I'm Just a Prisoner,* and *Sweet Feeling.* He wanted to hear those three songs. He wanted only those three songs. When we would try to play something else, he would pull his gun out and point it at us. We would start playing the songs again.

We sang those songs over and over for the entire performance. He stood by the stage and wouldn't let us come down. We sang until he had heard enough, and then he told us we could go. We were so angry because he held us until he was finished - not when we were finished.

I can tell you dozens of stories like this. I was doing a show in the hot summertime. I was sweating profusely when I left the stage. I was working hard trying to wipe off the sweat when I told my road manager, Leroy, to go to the office and get our money. We would always pick up the money, and then pay the band members on the way home.

Soon, Leroy came back and told me the boss wouldn't give him the money. He said that he wanted me to come to the office and get it personally. Now, there was no reason at all that this man would demand this hardship. I was dripping sweat and wanting to get out of that hot environment.

I walked back to the office and knocked on the door. The owner told me the door was open, so I walked in. I told him I wanted my money, so I could get out of there. I was hot and tired. He told me to calm down and relax. He asked me if I wanted a drink and what would I like. I told him again all I wanted was my money.

The man got up from behind his desk and walked toward me. He immediately grabbed me and tried to kiss me. I reached in my purse and pulled out my gun. I called him a fool and told him if he touched me again, I would blow him away. I told him to give me the money or else. He had cash on the desk. He took it and threw it at me and left me to pick it up as he walked out of the room. I was so angry I wanted to shoot his legs off.

I was down on the floor picking up bills from under the chairs, behind the desk, under the couch. I finally got it all picked up and went to the dressing room. I told my road manager to get us out of there. This is an example of what women had to go through to make it on the Chitlin Circuit.

I did a tour with James Brown. I opened for him for three days after he had a few rounds with the police. This affected the attendance at the shows. It wasn't as large as it had been. My record, *Young Hearts Run Free* had just released. James hadn't been exactly packing people into see him. I was singing my song and spotted James on my right. He was motioning with his hand across his neck to cut the song. Stop singing. He was letting me know it was time for him to come on.

I had thirty minutes, and I looked at my watch. I had five minutes left, so I ignored him. James was controlling everything, but this was my show, and I had five minutes to go, so I took the time.

James came on did all his usual gyrations. He was turning and twisting and doing the splits. When he got finished, he left the stage and expected people to run after him like they always did. There was only one very large lady following him. He turned around and said, "Oh Shit!" We laughed all the way to the next gig.

There were many nights on the Circuit that we couldn't finish our performances because of the fights that would break out. In the middle of our songs, people would run out of the place like it was on fire.

The Chitlin Circuit was no place for weak entertainers. It took guts to make the noise. We endured being robbed by the promoters that would hire somebody to steal from us after we'd been paid. Gun fights happened that would scatter the crowd heading for safety, and the show was over.

Probably the most graphic part of entertaining on the Chitlin Circuit was before Congress passed the Civil Rights Bill. We would stop for gas and be able to fill up okay, but if we wanted to go to the bathroom, we had to use the one marked for the "Coloreds." Bathrooms were marked, "Men, Women, and Coloreds." I was rebellious one time and went into the women's restroom. The attendant saw me and opened the door.

"Nigger," he said. "You know you don't belong in here."

We have gone to the woods to do our business because there was no restroom for the black folks. Hotels barred us, restaurants where we couldn't buy food, and every other hardship of man's inhumanity to man beat us down or tried.

I am thankful for my time on the Chitlin Circuit. It taught me how to sing in front of ten people or thousands. It made me tough as nails and to have the resolve to make it no matter how hard it was. I had beautiful people in my life that I will never forget. I am who I am today because of the time I spent working on the Chitlin Circuit. I would not trade the experiences; even though, I don't ever want to go back.

CHAPTER FOURTEEN

I Ain't Easy to Love

After divorcing Clarence, I was working in and out of the Chitlin Circuit. I worked in some really nice upscale clubs. My songs *Stand By Your Man, Mr. and Mrs. Untrue,* and *In the Ghetto. Stand By Your Man* and *In the Ghetto* were Grammy nominated songs. I also had a song called; I'm Just a Prisoner. *Sweet Feeling* was on the charts, and a song called *Evidence.*

My show was a really good one. I had seven musicians, and two background singers on the road with me. I was filling up clubs by myself, and life was good. Our band was four-piece rhythm, two horns, and the background singers. I've always been a light-hearted loving person, but life can really jerk you around sometimes, and you can lose the heart of hearts you were born with. Life has a way of doing that to us.

I began to be hostile after all the drama I had been dragged through. It didn't take much to make me angry and set me off. I learned how to handle difficult situations. I started drinking more and more. Getting drunk made me feel better, I thought. I was pretty much halfway inebriated most of the time because I didn't want to think about what I had been through.

I would drink to put myself to sleep, and drink to begin my day. Sometimes, I would start drinking around three o'clock in the afternoon if I was going to do a show that night. By ten o'clock it was show time at the club. Shows became routine, and didn't care much.

I could do my show because it was only another routine. I thought I had everything locked down in automatic mode. I have listened to those tapes I made years ago; they weren't that good because honestly, no one can do their best when they're under the influence of alcohol to the extent I was. I tried it, and it didn't work.

Then, I developed the attitude that I ought to kill myself. Forget that. I couldn't die, and so I live. I'm going to party, and I'm going to have myself some fun. I would order Champagne to my dressing room and throw in my drink of choice, Johnnie Walker Black. I loved Scotch and Courvoisier, and these drinks were always in my dressing room

I was for all practical purposes wasted by the time for my second show. I couldn't care less. We were traveling every day, and sometimes I would get home on Mondays. I had people beating my kids. The housekeepers were sometimes really good to the children, but some would treat them badly. I had to constantly get rid of housekeepers because the children would tell me they weren't being treat fairly, but I would always know better.

My children barely saw me. When I would get home, they would be in school, and I only got a few hours in the day to spend some good quality time with them. I missed so much of their lives, but what was I to do? The fathers of my children weren't helping them. Clarence sent a couple payments of four hundred dollars, or his court ordered support amount. After a couple, he never sent another dime. Joe was sending nothing to help support his kids, so I had no choice but to make the decisions I did.

I chose my music career. My children didn't want for anything. They had plenty of good and fashionable clothes to wear. They had shoes, lived in beautiful home, and had plenty of eat. We had the nicest cars, but all these material things I provided for them never could take the place of me.

My youngest son was five years old, and I was about to leave the house. He grabbed hold of my leg and began crying.

"Mommy, please don't go," he cried.

"Baby," I answered quickly. "I have to go to work. You have lots of toys I got for you. I bought a bike for you to ride. You have food. You have everything you need, and I have to keep working like I do to make sure you you're provided for."

"Mommy don't leave me," the little boy cried again, and this was breaking my heart.

Every time I went through a situation like that with the children, I drank more. That's all I knew to do. I didn't know how to handle it. I didn't know how to handle any of it, and I was thirty-five years old. I had been going through this hell since I was nineteen years old.

How many nineteen-year old girls have to go through this kind of drama? Most nineteen year olds are going to college. They've gotten their lives together, and most know what they want to study and become the rest of their lives.

My life was a hot mess at nineteen years old. I learned a lot from the street, and I have more wisdom than people may think I have. I can teach things now that I couldn't teach before because I had to experience what I am teaching to help people. When I tell you don't do certain things, I will also tell you what the results are going to be, and you can take it to the bank because I lived it. I'm not coming at you from a book; I'm coming at you from experience.

I had a long driveway at my house on Campbellton Road. I was about to leave, and Juno came running, screaming, and crying down the very long driveway. I had packed up the van, and we were getting ready to leave. Juno came down the road yelling,

"Mommy please don't leave me, please don't leave me."

"Stop", I told the driver, so he did.

I jumped out of the car and ran into the house. I got a bag together, threw some clothes in it and grabbed Juno. He was so happy that his tactics worked, and I was taking him with me.

The band loved Juno, and he was on tour with us. He was a happy little camper. Juno didn't seem to mind that we had enough alcohol in the dressing room to start a liquor store; he loved being with him momma. He ate all the potato chips and the candy. We kept him supplied with candy bars, and we had many toys in the dressing room.

One night, Juno was in the dressing room with me. I was holding him on my lap, and he'd slept a little bit. He was lying on the couch, and I thought he was asleep, so I sneaked out the door and onto the stage to perform. Juno wakes up and discovers that I am not anywhere in the room.

I had an unopened bottle of Johnnie Walker Black sitting on a table beside me. I'm up singing and singing. "I'm just a prisoner, your good loving, and the beat's going pop-bob-bob-pop-pop. The horns are playing and really getting into it. I'm singing away, and suddenly everybody's eyes left me. They burst out laughing all at once. I couldn't imagine what was going on. What sideshow had invaded the house? Well, it was Juno. He had walked out of the dressing room with my whole bottle of Johnnie Walker Black in his hand like he was drunk.

Juno sat on the steps where we were performing as calm as he could be. The only thing I could think to say was,

"Oh, MY GOD!"

Everybody in the audience was almost on the floor from laughing so hard. Juno was smiling. He was smiling with his Scotch in his hands. He sat the bottle down beside him and sat there grinning.

I let him sit on the steps for a while, but he was drawing too much attention, so one of the ladies behind the bar came and picked him up and set him on the bar. This was in the nineteen seventies, so we would be put in jail had it been now. The barkeeper took care of Juno until the show was over. We laughed so hard at the kid. He really was my little boo-boo.

I was on tour with Tyrone Davis. It happened in 1973. Tyrone was my good friend, and he was a great singer. He came from Chicago and had some real big hits. He and I became like brother and sister because we were on the road traveling so much together. You get to know someone when you're spending that much time with him.

Tyrone had a ten-piece band. He had a very large bus, and he kept a bodyguard with him at all times. The guy was not part of the band, and I suspected him to be a gangster. He had a gun all the time, and a shotgun in the bus. The promoters did not try to cheat Tyrone. He would send the gangster after his money, and the bodyguard always brought all of it back. Tyrone wasn't a man to play around. All of us entertainers have been slighted and cheated by promoters, but I doubt Tyrone ever lost a dime.

There was never anything personal between Tyrone and me before or after the shows. He loved to teach me, and he taught me a lot about how to save my voice by not talking too much during the daytime and much other useful information that made me a better entertainer and singer.

I bought this fancy souped up Cadillac. Its front end resembled a Rolls Royce. It had a white leather top, and I thought I really had something. I came driving up in my new car showing off, and Tyrone took me aside and said he wanted to talk to me.

"Candi, this is not you," Tyrone began. "What are you doing driving that gangster car?

"That's not a gangster car," I replied defiantly.

"Oh yes it is. You need to take that thing back where you got it and trade it in, and get something better than that ugly car. That's not your personality. You're a good person. You're one of those country girls, so you don't need to be riding around here looking like that. This car says there's another side of you that ain't pleasant. You need to take that thing back, and trade it in and get you a different kind of car."

"You make me sick, Tyrone. You're always in my business."

When I got off the tour, I took the car down to the Cadillac dealership. They had a big green limo on the lot. It was a beautiful green double limo that had been designed for Elvis Presley. Elvis said he didn't want that kind of car, so the car came back to the dealer, and they showed the limo to me.

The limo was equipped with a refrigerator, and seats that would swivel toward the open door and let you step out easily. The seats made a bed, and I was smitten by the beauty of this very large dark green limousine.

I traded my car that Tyrone Davis called a "pimp" car for a limo. When I did my next show with Tyrone, I showed the limo to him.

"That's what I'm talking about, sister. Now that's you girl. I am so proud of you," Tyrone said as he gave me a big hug.

Tyrone was grinning because I did everything to please him. We had one very lengthy tour together. Our tour promoter set us up in Oakland, California, and we started there. Roger Redding was my road manager then, and I opened for Tyrone.

I met the promoter when we got there. He was very friendly and talked a lot. He was comical and had a great sense of humor. He seemed to find me funny because he would laugh at everything I said. He found humor in everything. After our shows, he would come into my dressing room. He loved to bring Dom Perignon Champagne to me, or anything I wanted to drink.

We started hanging out together, and he was very nice to me. He paid me compliments. He called me "lady beautiful" and said I was the most beautiful woman he's ever seen. He flattered me, and I was flattered; maybe a little too flattered.

During the tour, I had a birthday, so he threw me a surprise birthday party in Oakland. He invited all his friends. About two o'clock in the morning after the show was over, and I was in my room, he called me.

"I need to see you right away," he said. "Can you come to my suite?"

"Yeah, okay, I'll be right there," I answered.

I got out of my show clothes and put some other clothes on and took off to his room. When I entered his suite, to my surprise, the place was loaded with people shouting "Happy Birthday, Candi." They started singing "Happy Birthday."

I was overwhelmed because I never expected that to happen to me in a million years. That was the first birthday party that was every given in my honor. As the party progressed, I was introduced to

Jimmy's friends. It was a culture shock; trust me. You would think I was on the set of *Shaft.*

There were mounds of Cocaine in little glass bowls and other drugs of all sorts. The place was drowned with alcohol. People were loud. I was there for about an hour, and I got so scared that the place would be crawling with cops, and my name would be ruined. I took off for my room.

The next morning, I mentioned it to him. He laughed.

"Never worry about the cops," he explained. "I have the police in my back pocket. You never have to worry about cops as long as you are with me."

He claimed to be part of the Mafia, and he said he owned a chain of funeral homes, which I never believed, and he also claimed to be loaded with money. I admit that he looked the part, and I was so naïve at thirty-five years old.

As a child, you never get away from the training you received at home. I was taught to believe that you take people's word and not to question it. Bishop Jewell had no street training, and mother knew nothing about life in places like Oakland, California, Los Angeles, or New York City. She had never experienced anything "uptown," so I wasn't familiar with any other way of life. I tended to trust everyone and believed whatever was said to me. I certainly wasn't familiar with conmen at least not at that time and on that level. If I had known then what I know now, I wouldn't have fallen for it.

I was seeing another guy in Atlanta at the time I was on tour. My girlfriend called me, and told me that she had seen him with another woman, and that really upset me. I got angry. I was sitting in my dressing room that night fuming. I was not my usual self, and I was trying to get the guy on the phone, but he wasn't answering.

Because I wasn't my fun loving, light-hearted self that I had been on tour, Jimmy asked me what was wrong with me. I told him how I felt, and I told him too much. Ladies, you have to understand that sometimes you can talk too much. You can open up your life to the wrong people, and they will take advantage of you. Don't open that door if you don't' want to get involved with someone. Only open those secret doors of life if you know somebody is right for you.

I opened the door. He began to hug me, and he said I could never do that to you. One thing leads to another, so I hooked up with him. He sympathized with me and acted like he was interested in me. He comforted me, but I did not hook up with him sexually.

What have I got to lose? I thought. *So what?* Let me caution everyone reading this book. Never date someone to get revenge. Revenge dating will always backfire on you, and it did to me.

I was planning a few one-night stands at best, and never planned on a full-blown relationship. Once a fire is lit, you can sometimes lose control. This is what happened in my case.

The tour lasted a couple of weeks and when it was over, I thought the affair would be over also. I was so very wrong. I was involved in something that was getting out of control. He blew up my phone every day. He told me over and over how much he missed me and wanted to see me.

I tried to ignore him because I wasn't physically attracted to him. He would never have been my choice for a lifelong partner. After three weeks of this constant badgering, he called me and said he was in Atlanta, and that he would love to take me to lunch. He said there were some shows coming up that he wanted to discuss with me.

He had lots of connections, and he knew how to promote shows as well as anybody in the business or better. I thought that I might need him in the future, and he was always so nice to me, that I told him I would come and meet with him for lunch. If I had only known what I was about to get into, I would have closed the door immediately, forever.

He came to my house the next day because I invited him. I had a lovely home on two beautiful acres of land in southwest Atlanta. I had three patios, a two-car garage, lovely back yard, and a barbecue where the housekeeper and I made meals and ate on one of the patios. It was a great time. I was a young fun loving, party going, and drinking lady. He was good company. I allowed him to spend the night and a few days later, he went back to Oakland, California. *It was good while it lasted* was my attitude.

Jimmy talked a lot about his connections with the gangsters and the bad boys in the Mafia. He told many stories about his relationship with these people, and the things they had done together. There was no doubt in my mind that he had another side to his personality, but I never dreamed how dark and dangerous that side would be.

Meanwhile, I was having trouble finding a good housekeeper that would be good for my children. There was a mother-in-law suite in the basement of my home that included a fireplace and two bedrooms. It had a nice kitchen, and practically everything you would desire for another family to be comfortable living downstairs. It was a nice place.

It was frustrating trying to find a good housekeeper to take care of my children while I was traveling, and I went through many of them. The last straw was when I came home from a trip, and the female housekeeper was drunk. At that time, the baby was about six months old. I inspected him, and it looked like his diaper hadn't been changed in days. His diaper rash was so bad; I had to take him to the doctor. This was just one incident of what these housekeepers were doing to me.

I had one housekeeper that had sex in my bed and didn't change the sheets. I needed somebody to come live with us that I could trust. I need someone badly. I had a nephew whose name was Jerry, and his wife was Diane. I knew them all of my life, and I knew they were trustworthy.

I had helped raise Jerry, so they were family. I contacted them and asked if they would be interested in moving into my home and take care of the kids while I was on the road.

My sons loved Jerry and Diane. Diane could really cook, and so they took care of my children, and it was a great setup. I could rest while on the road, do my job, and have complete peace of mind.

This was just too good to be true, and it was. Jerry's older brother came down from Cleveland to visit them. The brother saw where they were living and became insanely jealous. In fact so jealous that he decided to move in with me. He wanted to move in despite the fact that I was against it.

This man was no joke. He was a black belt in Karate, and he was mean and disrespectful. He came to visit and wouldn't leave. He was staying. When I protested, he threatened me and said the house was too big for me to be living in by myself, and that he was my nephew after all, and that he deserved to be there.

He invaded my home, and he talked about bringing his family to live there as well. He had four sons, and he was planning to bring them down from Cleveland. I told him there was no way I would let him do that.

He bullied me badly. I called the police and tried to get him out, but it was very touchy. He was Jerry's brother and my nephew as well. He was acting crazy, and I was between a rock and a hard place. I didn't know what to do. It is so strange what the police said when I called them.

"Just shoot him when he comes on the property," the cops told me.

I told them I put him out, but he was driving by my house and making threats, and they maintained that I should kill him. I said to myself, "I can't do that, he's still family. He's still my nephew, and I'm not going to hurt him."

While this was going on, I thought about Jimmy. His name was Jimmy Bullock. I called him and told him what was going on.

"I'll be on the next plane," he told me. "I'm going to straighten this out for you. Don't worry. They'll be gone in a few days."

It was so sad. It is so sad how family can become your worse nightmare. They are under the impression that if you become successful, you owe them something. I have known entertainers that have moved to other countries to get away from this type of mentality with family members. People who win the lotteries are sometimes broke within two years because of family.

Jimmy came to Atlanta and got rid of everybody. Jerry moved his family into and apartment, and his brother went back to Cleveland. I was so grateful. My kids were growing, and my oldest was fourteen years old at the time.

Jimmy hung around, and I really wanted him to leave. I wasn't in love with him, and he knew I wasn't, but he kept telling me how much he loved me. He wanted me to marry him. I kept telling him that I had just gotten divorced from Clarence Carter, and I wasn't mentally ready for a relationship. I wanted to be out there having fun.

Part of the problem was my youngest only five years old liked Jimmy. Jimmy was a big cut up and loved to laugh and play. He was like a big kid. My boy would crawl up on his lap and fall asleep, and Jimmy would carry him and tuck him into bed.

One morning, Jimmy woke up with this vision. He knew about my religious background. Sometimes people know about your background and will use it against you if you allow it.

Jimmy knew I was raised in church, so he knew I had a Spiritual upbringing and was into my faith. He was a con man. He told me that in the vision he was told that we were supposed to get married.

"God showed me in a dream that you were my wife."

"Man, you are joking," I laughed. "Come on now. I think you should go back to Oakland and let me think about it, okay?"

What happened next amazes me, but maybe someone reading this story won't be so amazed because you've had this same thing happen to you.

Jimmy gets up and goes to the kitchen. He makes breakfast and brings it to me on a tray to my bed. Bacon and eggs, grits, toast, jelly, and coffee were on that tray. The whole works.

"Jimmy, this is so nice, but I'm not hungry," I tried to explain without hurting his feelings.

"That's okay," he answered. "Drink your coffee."

God is my witness. I drank a few sips of that coffee, and I turned into another person within fifteen minutes. It was like part of my brain went to sleep. My whole personality changed. I became like a lamb to the slaughter. I could not disagree with him. I was calm and docile. I was totally under the control of this man.

"Get dressed," he said. "We're going to get married today."

I remember him helping me pick out the clothes. He went into my closet and picked out what he wanted me to wear telling me how nice I looked in each item I was wearing.

I still do not know what was in that coffee to this day. We got in the car and drove downtown. We went into a government building and found a judge. We didn't even get a blood test. I think it was a government building, and I think it was a real judge. I was in another world, so I can't swear to anything being legitimate.

I was out of it for about three weeks until Jimmy had his hooks into me. When I finally came out of the stupor, I cried for days because I was so depressed. The kids were depressed because Jimmy was not the nice, sweet, laughing, wonderful person neither the kids, nor I knew. He turned into the real Jimmy.

I felt like committing suicide again, and Jimmy completely took over my household. He bullied my children, so they would be in complete submission to him. He took over my business and became an uncontrollable monster. Most promoters were afraid to book me. My bookings fell off, and my band didn't know what to do. I began to lose everything. My band couldn't work with me because Jimmy was so mean and controlling. He was a liar pretending to be with the Mafia.

He claimed he was going to Quantico to become an FBI agent. It was indescribably horrible. I lost my house because I was behind on my payments. The reason? I couldn't pay my bills because he took all the money.

One incident that happened was with the band. I had to start playing on Army bases because the promoters couldn't handle Jimmy. He would ask for the money before I could even open my mouth, and before we got off the bus we were traveling in. He would ask for money, and then pull a gun on the promoters, and tell them he wanted every dime they owed me that night.

The promoters would tell him to pack up and get out of there because they weren't going to be threatened like that. They told him that he was asking for money before they set up or sound checked. It was crazy.

We had to get a promoter to get us on Army bases. Roger Redding started booking us in clubs on the bases because he said because all the other promoters had heard about her crazy controlling husband. We booked NCO clubs in various cities around the country. It was pretty smooth for a while, and each day I prayed that Jimmy wouldn't blow this, too. Well, he did.

We were in Oklahoma at a Non Commissioned Officers Club. We were playing the gig from ten o'clock p.m. to two o'clock a.m. The officer in charge told us we needed to be off the stage by one forty-five a.m. The people need to get back to the bases where they were stationed.

I closed down about one forty in the morning and said goodnight. The band was still playing. Jimmy was like a MC. When he would bring me on, he would say,

"Ladies and gentlemen, Candi Staton is in the house."

He would always say "goodnight" to them after the show was over. That particular night, it was one-fifty in the morning, and Jimmy started to sing. The sergeant came to my dressing room.

"Miss Staton," he said. "We need them off the stage, now."

I ran out and got the attention of my bandleader, Leroy, and told him to cut it. Jimmy was up on the stage clowning around. People were walking out anyway, and he got so mad.

When we got back to the dressing room, he cussed the band out, pulled a gun on the band, and wouldn't let them pack up the bus with their instruments. We were all standing around outside.

Jimmy was screaming as loud as his voice would let him and acting like a complete fool. I couldn't talk any sense into him. My fans came around for autographs, and Jimmy pointed his gun at my head. Everybody retreated and ran away for cover.

Finally, Jimmy put me in the car, and drove me to the hotel. We were almost to the hotel when he decided to pull the car over to the curb and made me get out. He then sped away leaving me beside the road.

This happened about three o'clock in the morning. A car full of drunken soldiers came upon me, and they asked me,

"Hey baby, where you going? Do you want some company?"

I am walking along and was about a block from the hotel. Jimmy is in my car, and I'm walking to my hotel at three a.m.

"Where do you want to go, honey? We'll take you wherever you want to be."

The boys were laughing. They were drunk. We were in front of a garage where people park cars all night, and the garage was empty. The streets were empty. There was not a soul anywhere to be found, and here I was so vulnerable to be raped or maybe even killed. It was a very scary situation.

Out of nowhere, this big black man comes out of the garage.

"What are you boys doing?" He said to them. "You better get on back to the base and leave this young lady alone."

"What are you doing out here alone by yourself?" He asked me.

"Well, my husband and I had a fight, and he put me out of the car."

"What kind of man would put a lady, who looks like you on the street at three o'clock in the morning especially in a military town? Anything could happen to you," he said. "Come on, I'll walk you to where you live. Where you staying?"

I walked with him up the long hill to the hotel. He went into the lobby with me, and then walked with me to my room.

"Look, take some advice from me and get rid of that man you're married to," he commented. "He doesn't care about you. Get rid of him, okay?"

"Yes sir, I will. I'm working on it."

"Make sure you do because if he keeps acting like this, you're not going to be around very long. Take my advice."

To this day, I believe that man was an angel. I believe God put that man there to save me from harm and to help me be strong about what needed to be done in my life.

Back in Atlanta, things were really awful, and they weren't going to get any better.

CHAPTER FIFTEEN
Victim of the Very Songs I Sing

Everybody was quiet driving back to Atlanta. The band members wanted to quit, so I got rid of everyone of them. I hired another band. This time, I got an all white band because no black band would work with me.

I put the Atlanta house on the market because Jimmy pretended that he wanted to go to Quantico, and he said that they would accept him in the academy. Things were very bad for us, and I didn't want to lose the house, but I put a For Sale sign in the front yard, and people were coming and looking over the house, and it was a quick sale.

While the house was on the market, we were rehearsing. I was so sick and tired of Jimmy. We were rehearsing in the garage, and the band was over-rehearsing. Roger called and told me he was working on some dates with Ray Charles. I wanted to get the band tight if we were going to be playing with the great Ray Charles.

We were moving to Reston, Virginia, but we had some shows to do before we actually moved over there. I was in the garage rehearsing when I heard the phone ringing in the bedroom. I had done many shows with Al Green, and he called to ask me how I was doing. We carried on a casual conversation for fifteen to twenty minutes.

Jimmy was in the garage trying to control the rehearsal because he tried to control everything. He looked around for me. When he realized I wasn't there, he walked into the house and found me in the bedroom talking on the phone.

"Who are you talking to?" He asked me.

"I'm talking to a friend."

"What friend?"

"Look, I'll be off the phone in a minute. Go on and rehearse the band. I'll be right there."

"Who are you talking to?"

"Al," I said to him. "Al, look. I'll call you. I'll call you back in a few minutes when I'm finished rehearsing, okay?"

"Al who?" Jimmy asked.

"Al Green. I was talking to Al Green."

Jimmy grabbed me by the shoulders and pushed me against the wall. He got very physical with me. He drew back his hand and slapped me. Oh, God, when he did that I could see nothing but red. All the evil, all the hurt, all the pain, all the times he'd embarrassed me, and every rotten thing he'd ever done to me came out of me.

Tina Turner had nothing on me when she attacked her ex – I kicked him. I pushed him. I tried to kick him in the balls, and I slapped him. I turned around backwards and kicked him, and I pushed him. He was a big heavy man, but I pushed him all the way to the door. I stepped back and ran into his stomach with my head and pushed him through the door. The whole door went down with him on top of it.

The band heard all the commotion going on, so they thought Jimmy was beating me up. Nope. They discovered I was beating

Jimmy up. He knocked all the hinges off the door, and he's lying there crying. This big old bully was whimpering and crying because his back was hurting him. He couldn't move. I tried to kill him that day.

The band ran into the room carrying sticks and rocks, whatever was loose they could find. They were going to do him in. They had knives and were going to rip him apart. When they got in the room, they found out that it was Jimmy doing the screaming.

"She done broke my back. She's broken my back. See, my back is broken," Jimmy cried to the boys in the band.

"Good," I said, and I kicked him in the head before I walked out the door. "Don't you ever put your hands on me again."

A few weeks later, my brother called.

"Why don't' you come on out to Reston," my brother Robert said. "I've got a house up here. I found the house the other day, and it's a beautiful home, Candi. Come on up here, and it's not too far from Alexandria. When you're on the road, I'll keep the kids for you because you know what you're going through with that fool. I don't know how in the world you got him, and I don't know how in the world you're keeping him. I wish you'd hurry up and get rid of him. I wish he'd go away. This fool is a tyrant. He's an uncontrollable idiot."

Things kept getting worse, so I moved to Reston and leased the beautiful house my brother was talking about. Soon after we moved in, my baby son got sick. He kept getting sicker and sicker. It turned out to be a trait of sickle cell anemia, and he would have coughing spells that awful. The weather in Reston was colder in the wintertime than Atlanta, and it didn't agree with him.

My brother, Robert, took really good care of my boy, and he loved Robert. He didn't miss me so much when Robert was there with him. *Young Hearts Run Free* was just out, and the news got to Warner Brothers how Jimmy was treating the promoters and DJ's, and how DJ's didn't want to play my records because they didn't want to deal with this fool in my life.

Female artists out there in those days seemed to always have a fool break into their lives. Female singers have undesirables hanging around because when you're in an area of music, you want to meet someone in that circle. If you're a teacher, you get involved with teachers. Doctors and nurses get involved with doctors and nurses.

In music, we move in the same direction, and a lot of times music people are not the most delightful beings to be involved with. Everybody knew I was blowing it. I remember when Gladys Knight had major problems in her relationship with the wrong guy. Aretha Franklin got hold of Ted White.

I am not a dumb person, and I'm not the kind of person that would pick up the first vagabond on the street in order to have a relationship. All those guys that dated me and eventually married me, were great guys but when they found out how much they could get away with, they took complete control and ruined what we had.

Warner Brothers was about to blow things up. Moe Austin was the President at that time, and he called for a meeting. They asked that Jimmy and I come out to Los Angeles and meet with them.

I won't forget what happened there. We sat around a table in the conference meeting room. Moe laid it all out.

"Jimmy," Moe began. "I've heard stories about the way you've been acting on the road. We've invested a lot of money in Candi Staton. I don't know whether you know this or not, but your behavior is running off many of our contacts and a lot of our DJ's and promoters. We're trying to build this lady into a superstar, and you seem to be doing everything you possibly can to break her down. Now, are you with her, or are you trying to destroy her? What are you going to do in her life if you aren't going to help her succeed? If you can't help her, we would appreciate it if you would move on out of the way because we're spending too much money on this woman to let you destroy everything we're trying to do. I am going to tell you now, Candi, you need a manager. You need to get this man off the road with you. That's all we can say or do about this situation. If you want us to keep you on our label, you have to get Jimmy away from you while on the road. We will drop you. That's all we have to say about it. If we hear about one more incident created by this man, we're done with you."

Jimmy looked at Moe dumbfounded. Then he said,

"Well, you know, I can stay in the house with the children. I don't have to go on the road with Candi. I can…"

"You do not by any stretch of the imagination even think about going on the road with this lady." Moe said emphatically. "You act like a fool every time you're out there with her. You need to stay at home and furthermore, why don't you get out of her life totally, and let her move on. Is it okay if we find new management, Candi?"

"Please do," I replied.

They sent several managers to me, and some of them were bad. I remember one particular manager who came to my house. I had a Chrysler at the time, so we went downtown Washington, D.C. to have lunch. He parked, and then got a ticket for parking in a restricted area. He took the ticket from under the windshield wiper, wadded it up, and threw it away. He got me in trouble, and I knew he wasn't going to manage me.

Warner Brothers introduced me to a man whose name was George Shiffer. He managed Ashford and Simpson and Mavis Staples. He managed a lot of different artists that were very highly rated. I knew Mavis from the Gospel music business. I felt that if George Shiffer was good enough for Mavis, he was good enough for me. He and I got along very well. I signed with George, and he took me over. George's manners on the road were impeccable. He was very good with the promoters, and he didn't like to show off his stuff.

I had to get a whole new band because they refused to go on the road with Jimmy. I left the band in Atlanta and hired a new one in Washington. Leroy was no longer my bandleader.

Jimmy would pull a gun on the band and me. He kept doing his dirty work. I found out he was pimping. He was a real pimp with prostitutes working for him. He had a fencing operation. Women would wear fur coats into shopping malls that had a lot of hidden pockets.

They were in the malls stealing merchandise and filling their pockets. They stuffed clothing in those coats and walked out. These were some very bad people. Jimmy didn't need his ladies anymore because he had my money, and he didn't want to lose it."

We finally got booked in Las Vegas with Ray Charles. This was probably the most exciting booking of my career so far.

"Guess what? We are booked for five days at the Aladdin with Ray Charles," Roger told me.

This was the beginning of the end of my life with Jimmy. It was exciting to see my picture on billboards with Ray Charles and the Supremes. There were also many postcards announcing our coming to Vegas.

In the hotel, the Supremes were given a small room to perform in, and I was placed in the main auditorium with Ray Charles. I was given a fabulous suite on the twentieth floor. Ray sent his road manager to my dressing room with a message.

"Tell Candi if I wasn't blind, I would have come to her dressing room by now to say hello." That was the second night of our show.

This was not a personal issue. I had been to many superstars' dressing rooms, and had been rejected and treated so badly. I had been ignored to the extent that I swore I would never go to another superstar's dressing room. I would do my job and get the hell out of there.

I decided that I would never go to Ray's dressing room. I would say hello to him before I would leave, but he was so nice.

"Ray sent me to tell you this," his road manager said.

My goodness this was so different. Ray Charles was different.

"Okay, where is his dressing room?" I asked while picking up my purse.

I followed Ray's manager to the dressing room. When I got in there, I hugged Ray Charles, and I stayed with him. We talked all evening while we drank Amaretto and coffee. He always had this drink before he went on stage. There was a large thermos sitting next to him.

"Pour out some Amaretto and coffee," he said. "Come on and have a drink with me."

I had a drink, and we sat there and talked.

"I'm coming here an hour early, so meet me here every night," Ray said. "We're going to have a conversation every night. You just hang with me until we get ready to go on stage. Is that okay with you?"

I told Ray that I would be there every night. We met in the dressing room for the rest of the week. We sat and talked about everything. He would tell me all about the troubles he had through the years and about his struggles on the Chitlin Circuit. We laughed about how we were both in the Chitlin Circuit. Ray told me all about the movie that was coming out about his life and career.

One night we were sitting and talking and Ray said to me,

"You know you're a female Ray Charles, right?"

"What do you mean? I curiously asked.

"You are a female Ray Charles. I'm part country, I'm part blues, I'm part Gospel. I'm all of these music genres, and so are you. That's what makes our songs feel like they feel. That's what I am, and you're a female Ray Charles. You know what else? You do a great job at it."

"Ray, that is the most wonderful compliment anybody has ever given me in my entire lifetime. Thank you so much," I said as I walked over and hugged him. "I'll see you after the show. Have a great show. I'll be back tomorrow night."

"Same time?" He asked.

"Yep and same place."

It was Friday night, and we were near our last show. I knew Jimmy was probably seething, and he wasn't acting up in Las Vegas. He was distant and angry because he hated that I was spending so much time with Ray Charles. What could he say? He couldn't say or do anything about it. This was Ray Charles.

I had not been able to see Ray's show in its entirety. I had seen bits and pieces from the dressing room, so I made up my mind that I was going to the show because this was the last night, and I wanted to see his entire performance.

About halfway through the show, I saw Jimmy come in and start looking around. I knew he was trying to find me. I ignored him. I acted like I didn't see him, and he never spotted me; even though, I was sitting on the second row of the left side in plain view.

I walked out with the crowd when the show was over. Jimmy was standing by the door, and he was shaking with anger.

"Let's go upstairs," Jimmy said.

"We took the elevator up the suite, but nothing was said between us. He opened the door to the suite, and then pushed me through the open door. He began to shake me, and then threw me on the bed with his fist balled up. He began hitting me on the back. He choked me and was screaming,

"When you see me looking for you bitch, you better never ignore me. Oh, no, I'd make too much noise if I shoot you," Jimmy said as he took out his gun and pointed it at me.

Instead of pulling the trigger, he grabbed me and carried me to the balcony. He held me over the rail and threatened to drop me. He dared me to speak or even cough. He said that if I made a sound he would let go of me. I looked down.

"Oh, my God," I said when I got the nerve to speak. "Jimmy, have you forgotten were we are? We're in Las Vegas where the real Mafia is located. They own this hotel, Jimmy. Can you imagine what's going to be on the front page of the paper in the morning if you happen to do this stupid thing?"

I was looking down, and the cars looked like matchboxes with wheels on them.

"It will be all over the news, Jimmy. They're going to report that last night the husband of Candi Staton throws her from the balcony of the Aladdin Hotel. Jimmy, they will find you, and they will kill you. Are you ready to die? You won't get away with this. Go ahead. Drop me. My life is a living hell being with you anyway."

Jimmy pulled me over the rail and stood me up on the balcony. We walked into the room. I lay down on the bed. I was exhausted emotionally and physically. I could feel the veins pulsating in the back of my head. My stomach was in a knot, and I was shaking. I was going to sleep, and there was a peace that came over me. I don't know why or how, but I was at peace. It was a Godly peace.

Scripture verses started popping into my head, and things I thought that I have been taught and believed all my life.

The Lord is my Shepherd; I shall not want. He makes me to lie down in green pastures; he leads me beside the still waters. He restores my soul; he leads me in the paths of righteousness for his name's sake. Yea, though I walk through the valley of the shadow of death, I will fear no evil: for thou art with me; thy rod and thy staff they comfort me. Thou prepares a table before me in the presence of mine enemies: thou anoints my head with oil; my cup runs over. Surely goodness and mercy shall follow me all the days of my life: and I will dwell in the house of the Lord forever.

These verses began to repeat over and over in my mind like a broken record, and through the fear, peace came over me, and I strangely fell asleep. Jimmy's gun was pointed at my head when I went to sleep. I know it now without any doubt that God was in the room.

"When you're ready to kill me," I told Jimmy before I fell asleep. "Go ahead and murder me."

I don't know when Jimmy left the room but when I woke, he was gone. I got out of the bed and went to the bathroom. I didn't even wash off my make-up. I still had my clothes on that I was wearing when I fell on the bed. I took a shower and dressed for the day.

I heard a key turn the lock on the door. Jimmy came in as though nothing had ever happened. He was laughing, joking, and trying to tell me a joke. I had ordered breakfast through room service and was getting ready to eat.

"Where's my breakfast?" He asked. "You knew I was coming back, so why didn't you order me some breakfast?"

"Oh well, order your own breakfast."

I never mentioned what happened the night before, and I was acting normal the best I could.

Last night I made up my mind that I have to get away from him if I want to live. I made some plans about how I can leave him, and I am going to leave him.

The last performance was upon us, and I did what I had been doing every night before the performances. I went to the dressing room for an hour, and I talked to Ray. I never saw him for a very long time.

David Gest, who was married to Liza Minnelli called me when I was in Atlanta and asked me to be on the "Toys for Tots" show in New York City. The year was 2000. I had done the show many years before, and David said he's always been a fan, and that he wanted me on the show in Madison Square Garden.

There were twenty top singers on the program that night, and I was privileged to have been invited to sing with such a prestigious group of stars. I was told that Ray Charles was there, and I saw him.

I was with my son, Marcus, and my publicist, Bill Carpenter. We went to find Ray's room. I knocked on the door.

"Who's there?" Somebody screamed from inside the room.

"Candi Staton. Tell Ray it's Candi Staton, and I want to see him."

"I'll be right out as soon as I put my pants on. I want you to walk me to the stage," Ray exclaimed.

I told Ray I'll be here when you're ready. That was the last time I saw my friend alive, and I miss him. I miss his warmth. When he got sick, I began to pray for him. He only lived a couple more years.

Jimmy and I went back to Reston. All I could think about was how I could get rid of the monster. In the evenings, I walked through the neighborhood for exercise. I prayed while I was walking and asking God how in the world I was going to survive.

For the first time in years after I rejected God and was mad at the church, I now found myself laying all my problems on the Lord. I was realizing that God was not my problem. Dealing with people was my problem, so I was calling on God and asking Him to help me get rid of the man.

It's amazing how God knows how to run you back home to Him. He will put the worse people in your life sometimes to bring you back. He never changes, and He never leaves His post. He's always there where you left Him. He will allow the enemy to oppress you in order to get your attention, and let you know you've come to the end of your rope. When that happens, all you can do is look up and call on God when you feel it is the last mile you can run, and life is over.

For weeks I was walking the neighborhood and talking to the Lord. I asked Him for a way out. I said, *God get me out of this. I can't do this by myself because I don't know how. Jimmy has threatened to kill me if I ever leave him. He said he would kill me, kidnap the children, or kill the children. I think he's capable, Lord. If I ever needed you, God, I need you now.*

I had a dream that night. I was running, and Jimmy was behind me trying to catch me. He had two horns coming out of his head, and I was fleeing for my life. I then heard a voice say, *Go home, Go home.*

I woke up dripping wet with sweat and so wet that I had to get up and draw a bath wondering what that dream could possibly mean. My mother in Alabama was always praying for me, and she called me. She had heart disease, and she told me she was in the hospital and wanted me to come home. She had another heart attack, so I booked my flight and stayed with several days until they released her from the hospital.

Fall was beginning, and I was missing my children that I left at home in Reston. It was a beautiful day, and we were sitting on the porch. Mr. Johnson, a longtime family friend drove by the house. He saw me sitting there, so he drove up and rolled down his window.

"Hey there girl, what are you doing home?"

"What are you doing now?" I asked after exchanging some small talk.

"Well, I'm on my way to put up a for sale sign on some land I own down the road." I have five acres of property on the main highway."

"How much do you want for it?" I asked. "Can I ride down with you and take a look at it?"

As got near the property, I could see it was very beautiful acreage. It was surrounded by rolling hills, and a lot of beautiful trees and was really a nice layout for a place to build a beautiful home.

"I'll take it," I said to him quickly.

"What?" He asked strangely.

"You would be surprised, Mr. Johnson," I laughed while writing out the check.

I signed the deed a few days later, and I owned land two miles from my mother's house.

I returned to Reston and worked two more weeks, and then went back to Alabama. I was introduced to a contractor, who built beautiful homes made from cedar. I owned a cedar house.

The house was beautiful and almost perfect sitting the woods. I picked the design I wanted, went to the bank for a loan, and started building the house. Because I was married, the bank needed Jimmy's name on the loan. I hated this.

"Can't you just, can't you, why can't I do this loan by myself?" I told the banker.

"Are you married or not?" He asked.

"Yes, I am."

"What is your name?"

I told him James, but my husband had changed his name. He

had legally changed his name from Jimmy Bullock. I then gave him my last name, and he said he was going to put down Mr. and Mrs. James.

The loan went through, and I had picked out the plans to suit my needs. The contractor proceeded to start building the house. It only took two or three months, and the house was about ready.

Jimmy was not happy, but he wasn't saying much because he had nowhere to go. Somehow I knew that God was answering my prayers and taking care of my problem. I told him we were moving to Alabama, and you should have seen his face. There was zero he could do, and I knew God was at work. Don't ever think God is not looking out for you. In every area of your life, He is there watching over you.

We packed up before the house was ready, so I could go down and pick out carpeting, and all the other things that are necessary in a house. We were back in the Colony at Hanceville, Alabama. I rented a large storage area to keep my things until the house was finished, and we could move in.

My mother's house was very small. She only had two bedrooms, a tiny kitchen, one bathroom, a living room, front porch, and a small back porch. Jimmy and I stayed in the second bedroom, and I had folding cots to put in the living room for the children.

Jimmy was beyond uncomfortable. He was restless and confused at living in an environment that was strange to him. This was real country living. My stepfather, Mr. Marsh, raised chickens, hogs, and he had a garden. My cousin lived next door, and the children would go play with their cousins. They did everything together, and they became like brothers and sisters. They went fishing, and my cousin, Bertha Lee, let the kids spend the night at her house sometimes.

I enrolled the kids in school, so everybody was getting settled except Jimmy. I knew so many people there. I would leave and go to my aunt's house, stay over at my cousin's place, and hang out with friends. Jimmy had nobody to visit because nobody liked him. He would try to joke and laugh, but they looked at him like he was a fool or somebody from outer space.

He eventually made a couple of friends that he drank with. I couldn't imagine how uncomfortable he was; yet I enjoyed every minute watching him squirm. I know God was at work because you reap what you sow. He was so miserable. My mother didn't like him at all. When he tried to find favor with her, she would look at him and roll her eyes. She could see straight through him.

"Where in the world did you meet this Devil?" She asked me one day. "He's evil. He's no good, and I'm going to pray him away from here."

Jimmy couldn't manipulate her. Country people are difficult to manipulate. He found himself in a completely different world than he'd ever experienced.

The house was nearly finished when his emotional battle came to a boiling point. Jimmy couldn't take anymore country - fide living. The dark side came out that had been hidden for nearly three months.

My oldest son, Marcel, wasn't living with us. I had to send him away because the older he got, the more fights he got into with Jimmy. Marcel was eighteen years old, and I knew he was trying to kill Jimmy. I sent him to live with his father in Birmingham, and he was still there. If Marcel was there, a murder would have taken place.

Marcus, Terry, and Mr. Marsh had gone fishing. It was a Saturday morning. I had been reading Norman Vincent Peale's book on positive thinking. I wrote thoughts on yellow notepaper, and put it in my wallet, so that every time I opened it, I could see the notes. I looked at it every day, and this particular day I was holding the note in my hand and reading it. It read, *Nothing is going to happen today that God and I can't handle.* I was repeating it over and over.

I cooked breakfast that morning for everybody. My mother had just gotten up. I was cleaning the tiny house, and Jimmy asked me if I would come with him down to the house I was building. I followed him to the van we used for that road. I was sitting in the driver's seat, and I proceeding to start the car. All of a sudden, I had this overwhelming feeling that I shouldn't go down there with him.

"Can we talk here?" I asked Jimmy. "I'm not going to the house."

"How many times have I told you I will never divorce you?" He said.

I asked him for a divorce a couple of day's prior, and he was pondering over my request.

"How many times have I told you I will never divorce you? I will kill you first. Don't every bring up this subject to me again."

"Oh yeah, I am going to divorce you, Jimmy, and there's nothing you can do about it. I married you against my will. I put up with your crap for two years, and I'm no longer going to put up with it. I am done with this evil because of your diabolical manipulations and hatred. You have embarrassed me. You cuss me out, and I've been afraid every day of my life since I met you. Yes, I am going to divorce you, and I'm not afraid of you anymore."

Jimmy got out of the van and very calmly walked to the house. He told me to wait because he would be right back. He was gone for about five minutes and came out of the house. He had a gun and pointed it at me.

"I will kill you first. You are not going to divorce me. I will kill your mama, your stepdad; I will kill all your children right in front of your mother. Maybe a heart attack will take that bitch out. I don't like your mama, and I don't like your family. I don't like nobody. I hate all of you. I don't care what happens today as long as I kill your ass."

My first impulse was to run and save my life, but I heard this voice saying, *Stop. He can't kill you because I won't let him.*

My cousins were next door washing cars. They saw him coming towards me with the gun. They started screaming for me to run because he's got a gun. The van was running, so I quickly put it in gear and pulled ahead about one hundred feet and stopped.

My six-year old was running to me and passed on the side where Jimmy was holding the gun. He could have killed him right then. I rolled down the window, and he came up to me pointing the gun.

"I'm going to kill your ass today," he said.

"Oh no you're not," I told him. "God is not going to let you."

My poor sick mother was on the porch screaming at him.

"Leave my child alone. In the name of Jesus, you can't kill her. You better stop now and leave her alone."

I opened the door with no fear. I was absolutely unafraid of him.

I got out of the van, and he hit me across the face with the gun. He slapped me. He pushed me, and I pushed him.

"I'm going to the house, Jimmy, and I'm going to call the police. I am not afraid of you anymore."

Jimmy jumped in the van and drove away. He threw my gun into the ditch. He didn't own a gun, and it was my gun pointing at me the entire time he had a gun. Later that evening, the boys and their friends found the gun in the ditch and brought it back to me.

I called the police. When they came, I told them what happened, described the van, and gave them the license plate number. It took the police a while to get out there to me, and I knew Jimmy would be halfway to Louisiana by then. He had a credit card and used that to pay for his travel expenses.

I shudder when telling this story to think about what could have happened to my baby. My baby boy could have been shot and killed, and my mother would surely have had a fatal heart attack. God's protection was upon us. There was nothing the Devil could do. He was helpless because the very thing he used to control me was gone. I had no fear. The fear I felt was broken. Satan had no more power. He knew the game was over but wait. There's always one more thing. Jimmy's name was on the loan, and he had to sign before we could close.

The closing on the house was set up and ready, but we had that one situation. Jimmy wasn't around. After he had been gone about three months, he called constantly. He was so annoying that I wouldn't answer the phone. I had to pull the phone out of the wall to keep him from calling, so we could sleep.

I went to the bank to close the house. They asked me where my husband was, and I told them that we were separated and not getting back together. They wanted to know if we were married, and I had to say yes because I couldn't produce any divorce papers to show otherwise. I kept insisting that we will never be back together, and he won't pay the loan. It didn't matter. I was stuck.

The contractor wanted his money. I paid my attorney to close the deal up front. The bank kept waiting.

"Can you get him back to close?" My Attorney asked. "Will he come back to you, so you can close this house?"

"You don't understand," I answered. "The man tried to kill me several times, and I barely escaped with my life."

The Attorney convinced me that I needed to get him back because the contractor was getting very, very angry and restless. He could take the property. Here I was again in another mess.

A tour came up in London with the Stylistics, and Jimmy was talking that tour up before he left. We were putting a tour together, and he wanted to go to London and had applied for and received his passport. He kept on calling. Finally, I talked to him.

"I'll come home and sign for the closing if I can go to London with you," he said over the phone.

Jimmy came to the Colony. He stayed in a hotel and also stayed some nights with a friend in Birmingham until we closed the house. He came back to the house, and we resumed a tiny relationship. I hated his guts. I so badly hated him, and I don't like using that word because it is so strong, but I did hate him so much that I couldn't stand the sight of him.

The contractor was paid in full. We went to the storage area, picked up the furniture and moved in the house. Jimmy was so happy to be back. A couple of weeks later, we went on tour, and Jimmy was with us.

I don't think I ever knew Jimmy's real name. His birth name was Jimmy Bullock, but I knew him as Jimmy James. He got his name changed to James, so that he could get a passport. We were not getting along at all.

When we arrived in London, the Promoter got us a suite. Jimmy ordered Dom Perignon every day. At restaurants, he ordered the most expensive food on the menu. I was a nervous wreck the entire tour. My manager, George Shiffer, was with me. When we got on the bus to make the performances, Jimmy would pick at me constantly and openly.

There were two bedrooms in the suite, and I refused to sleep with him. One night, he got drunk and raped me. I lay there and took it. One night on the road, the bus stopped at a rest stop, and Jimmy got off. He got into it with a bunch of punk rockers. It was an ugly scene. When he got back on the bus, he was angry with the background singers, my manager, the band, and everybody else because no one got off the bus and helped him fight.

My background singers were traveling with me, and they were called F-360. They also traveled with Luther Vandross. They watched this whole episode and wondering.

"Girl, how can you deal with this man?" Fonzie said, who was one of the background singers.

"It won't be long, it won't be long," I replied. "As soon as I get home, I'm going to get rid of him."

The tour finally ended, and little did I know that I made no money. I got absolutely nothing for the whole tour because Jimmy burned it all up on food and drinks.

I rested for a day after we got back home in Alabama. I drove over to Cullman and filed for divorce. When I got home that afternoon, I found that my sister had come down to visit our mother. Mom had another heart attack. I told my sister about the dilemma I was in, so she told me to come to Nashville with her, and we could leave the next day.

I told everybody I needed a break, so I left with my daughter and baby son. The other three boys stayed behind with mother. She was well enough after her slight heart attack to manage, and they were no trouble to look after.

In Nashville, I rented an apartment and furniture and set up housekeeping with my two kids in tow. Jimmy was at the new home by himself. The electricity got cut off, the water was turned off, and he had no food. I was told that he went to somebody's house every evening.

In the country, people will feed you if you are sitting around long enough while they're cooking dinner. They would call him sometimes, and tell him to come over and have some supper, and he was glad to hear that. He would go and eat with people until he finally got tired of it. He saw that I wasn't coming back, so he wrote a bad check to Delta Airlines and flew to Oakland, California. You could write a check back then, and they would take your word it was good. There wasn't any digital way to process the check.

Jimmy took a whole lot of my stuff with him. He took my music that Warner Brothers had written for orchestras, and he also had to do something really stupid before he left. What good was that music to him? I reasoned it didn't matter as long as I was completely done with him once and for all.

When the time came for the divorce to be signed, he called me, and I answered the phone.

"Jimmy, you have a warrant for your arrest. If you come back into this town, they're going to arrest you for that bad check you wrote to Delta Airlines. I am going to inform them that you are in the area."

Jimmy didn't show up for the final court date. I got the divorce by default, and I got the house and everything else that belonged to me. I stayed single for three more years.

Relationships are impossible to maintain when you're not with the right person. Sometimes, they are hard enough to make-work when you are with the right person. You can't imagine the pain and agony when you're hooked up with the wrong person unless you've been there. I hated walking on landmines in my own home. It's a literal war zone.

Home is supposed to be a place of safety, commitment, and love. It's a place of serenity and joy but when get to the point where you have to quote verses from Psalm 91 to ten Hail Mary's just to walk through the door because you don't know if you're going to meet Dr. Jekyll or Mr. Hyde. It is pure torment.

I have had my share of crazy relationships to last anyone a life-time. Life goes on and as my record says, *Life Happens.* As sure as the sun shines in the morning, you will inevitably meet someone else in another suit. The same man, a different smile, a different face, a different size and color, but the same fundamentally flawed person.

I asked myself so many times, *What's wrong with me? Why do I get into these types of relationships with the men in my life?*

The answer is the circle I was living in. It is the flaw of being an entertainer. How naïve can you get? The fame and riches are great, but how naïve are all these people including myself?

I am so much like my mother. I am too helpful. My mother and father stayed married until he passed away. Daddy was drunk most of the time, and he wasn't faithful to my mother. She still treated him right. She cooked, she cleaned, and she washed his clothes. She was always a wife and mother first, and I suppose I learned my domestic habits from her. Times have changed, and I just read a book entitled, *Why Men Love Bitches.*

I bought the book primarily because I wanted to see how much times have changed. I was doing wrong to try and correct it. I was living in a different era than most people are living in now. I can't retrain myself how to act in this age. I am still sort of stuck in the past as to how I was treated and raised as a child. It is difficult to shake.

I was completely shocked when I read that book. Men were treated badly, but they couldn't stay away from the woman – the worst women in the world. The men were disrespected terribly, but yet they still love those bad women. I wasn't raised like that. For the life of me, I can't behave towards people like that. I can't talk to people like that, and I can't act with that kind of disrespect. Yet, I was handled the same way those men were by their women in that book.

I don't get it, and I'm not a passive rug either. I'm not someone you can walk over whenever you feel like it. I do have some fire in me. You can't walk over me. I'll take all I can stand, but I will react when things get out of hand. I don't stick around, and I will leave for my own safety. I'm not going to let anyone kill me, and I'm not going to kill anybody. You can always leave. I've been tempted to do that, but when it seems I've taken all I can take, God always steps in and gives me strength to carry on.

I am writing this book, so others can see what I've gone through and gather strength from my experiences, so they can make it thorough their own trials and tribulations. You can come through with more strength and faith to keep moving forward because I know you can.

I was in a marriage that never was. I went through all that hell – all that mess, and I was never married to Jimmy. A fake Justice of the Peace married us. We had a fake marriage license. I divorced a man I wasn't married to. Think on that for a minute. When I finally learned that we were nowhere on the books as being husband and wife, I had to laugh. It was really funny to me. I came through strong whether I was married to that man or not, I still came through strong.

CHAPTER SIXTEEN

I Ain't Got No Where to Go When the Music Stops

I want to make a statement before I start the next Chapter of my life. I have learned so much. I've learned that sometimes you keep drawing the same spirit to you because your soul is subconsciously looking for that familiar spirit that has dominated your past. Seeds are planted, and then reproduce after their own kind.

This is why we keep drawing the same kind of kindred spirits that will mistreat you in the same way you've become accustomed. Do you ever wonder why you get so disrespected? It is because you soul and mind make you disrespect yourself. Disrespect is drawn to you, and you are not remotely aware it is happening.

Painful experiences get into your soul. The same people keep showing up because what is inside of you comes out. It is repro-ducing itself over and over again. This is why you get the same treatment every time. Don't let the same hurts control your future.

Hurt people hurt other people. Have you ever heard the expression, "You hurt the ones you love?" The same beat goes on and on, and you can't seem to shake it because it's embedded in your soul. Oftentimes, we need therapy. We need to talk the problems out. We need to face the things that we previously were incapable of facing. We need to take off the mask that we've been wearing, pretending things are fine, and everything is okay; everybody loves you.

Everybody doesn't love you. You have to love yourself, and sometimes we get so hurt by things that have taken place and unfolded in our lives that we think they are normal. Those familiar things that have dominated your persona seem normal when they are abnormal to everyone else. Getting hurt over and over, people coming into your life mistreating you is modus operandi. If people are not abusing you, you feel displaced, unaccepted, and empty.

It is a mystery how you can feel abused when someone is not screaming at you and disrespecting you. That is the result of what is inside of you drawing those feelings back to you, so that you feel normal again. It sounds crazy, but I know it to be true in my own life, and in the lives of others who are relating to my story.

Jimmy James is gone, and everything is back in order. Marcel moved home to live with us. Three teenage boys are living in my house, and a preteen girl. I am free and working regularly. George Shiffer booked a tour with Teddy Pendergrass for two weeks. It was a wonderful tour. I was kicking butt and taking names.

One night when Teddy arrived at the auditorium, the crowed was chanting, "More, more, more, more, more."

The next night, Teddy Pendergrass was on the front row to see what he had to follow. It was funny to me, but I intended to put on a show, and I did. I saw him sitting on the front row, so I went for it. Man, we did such a show that night, and it was amazing. Teddy came on behind me and lighted up the crowd. I was having the time of my life.

I was done with the Chitlin Circuit, and I was now on the big concert circuit with the big-named artists on the big time stages.

Universal Attractions that booked all the superstars was now booking Candi Staton. *Young Hearts Run Free* was still a big hit. Warner Brothers began trusting me to co-produce with top producers. One of them was Jimmy Simpson, who is Valerie Simpson's brother.

I am recording on contract with Sigma Sound Studios in New York City with Jimmy Simpson. Roberta Flack was recording with Jimmy Simpson and I got to know her. She was very close to Ashford and Simpson.

I was living in an apartment on 7th Avenue in New York City. George was creating a new image in me, and he was working very close with Warner Brothers to get it done.

When I was not on tour, I was working gay clubs and straight ones. I only needed my sound tracks for disco, and I was a happy camper. I was working all the time at the Garage and Studio 54.

My children were living in our house in Alabama, but I was practically in New York most of the time. I would go home occasionally, but I considered myself a New Yorker. George Shiffer began asking the DJ's to announce that I was from New York when they would introduce me. That never set well with me because I was still an Alabama girl.

Occasionally, I would bring my kids to New York to stay with me in my small apartment. The kids did not like New York City at all. There was no place for them to play outdoors, and it was not normal for them. They missed their friends and their grandmother. They loved mama's cooking, and they had the best of all worlds in Alabama. It was especially important for them to have the adult supervision at home with them at all times. Of course they lived in a spacious and beautiful home with lots of property.

My oldest son, Marcel, was in charge of the home. I would call him everyday and give my instructions. They had opportunities to do whatever they wanted, and they enjoyed that freedom. The boys were old enough to drive, and all three had their licenses. They had their own cars, and I provided a charge account at a local clothing store where they could go shopping whenever they needed anything. My mother would cook dinner for them, and it was a good place at the time.

The only major problem I had was Jimmy. He was stalking me, so George Shiffler hired a bodyguard to travel with me. He was very good at what he did. He worked formerly for Michael Jackson, and he was with me everywhere I would go. He had a room next to mine in the hotels.

We were in Chicago at a disco club that was completely packed with patrons, who came to see my show. I spotted Jimmy trying to make his way to the stage. I gave my bodyguard a signal that he had given me that was special in case Jimmy came around.

I was on my last song of the night when Jimmy was headed towards me. I signaled to my bodyguard, and I did not finish the song. My bodyguard grabbed the two-track tape from the DJ, and we headed out the back door. We jumped in the limo and headed straight for the hotel.

Somehow, Jimmy found out where I was staying, but we were one step ahead of him. My bodyguard and I exchanged rooms. He called my room, and the bodyguard answered, and threatened Jimmy's life, and I didn't see him again on that trip.

George Shiffler and I were together in Philadelphia doing a promotion for a tour. The bodyguard was not with us on this trip, and I don't remember why, but it may have been because we didn't think we would need him. Jimmy had not bothered us for quite some time.

We were ready to leave our hotel in Philadelphia, and I came downstairs to check out. Jimmy was standing in the lobby waiting for me. He never touched me, but he did say he only wanted to talk to me.

I stared at Jimmy, and these thoughts drifted through my brain. *After all these years, what a total waste of time he was. How did I ever get involved with a low-life, unattractive, evil person like this man is?*

I could not have disliked Jimmy James more than I did. I looked at him with all the hate and disgust a person could feel.

"What do you want Jimmy?" I asked him. "Get a life because I don't want you in mine. I will have you arrested if you bother me anymore."

"I just wanna talk to you," he said. "Can you come outside?"

"Are you out of your mind?"

George was coming down the stairs. He couldn't believe Jimmy was standing there.

"Do you want me to call the police?" George said.

"Yes, George, call the cops." I said loudly.

George called the police, and you should have seen Jimmy running out of the hotel. I let my bodyguard go because I had no need for him anymore. I never again saw Jimmy James, or whatever his name was, to this very day.

I stayed in New York for a year. George Shiffler and I had become very close and personal friends. George was a Corporate Attorney, but he had a very bad drinking problem in spite of his credentials. I hung with him almost every day, and I attribute becoming an alcoholic to hanging around too much with George. Up until the time we became so close, I was only a social drinker.

George had an apartment in Los Angeles. I would travel to L.A., and he put me up in a hotel suite for two months. I was scheduled to record with Chaka Khan's producer, Bod Monaco. We were recording an album, *Music Speaks Louder Than Words.*

I had recently recorded Young Hearts Run Free, and David Crawford was scheduled to produce my next record, but he got really horrible. He didn't want to produce another record on me. He thought that Young Hearts Run Free was such a big record that he should have sung it.

David Crawford was an aspiring singer. He was a very good musician, but he didn't have a voice good sellable enough to make records. How could a man sing *Young Hearts Run Free* anyway? He was very jealous, and his competitive nature caused him to tell Warner Brothers that he would not produce another record on me. He was so cantankerous that we had to find another producer, and I started coming down on the charts because we were doing a different genre of music.

Music Speaks Louder Than Words contained songs like *Listen to the Music* and *Nights on Broadway.* Some of those songs did fairly well on the charts. I was also doing a bunch of disco gigs. When I wasn't in the studio recording, George and I would go out to the finest restaurants in New York and Los Angeles. I was having the time of my life. We attended special events and many promotional parties in L.A. Warner Brothers Records really were fond of me. We called them Moe and Joe Smith and Moe Austin.

CHAPTER SEVENTEEN

Young Hearts Run Free

In spite of the fact that Warner Brothers was extremely happy with my performance as an artist, I was getting tired of city life. I wanted to go home. I had been on the road for more than two years, and I wanted to be with my kids. They needed me, and I needed them.

One day, I got so fed up with the life that I was living that I decided to take off. I left my post cold turkey. George was angry with me, but I couldn't care less. I had enough partying and jet setting. I needed some peace in my life. I longed for the laid back lifestyle I used to live in the country in Alabama. I needed the balance. I needed to settle back into myself because I was losing the woman I used to be. I was drinking every night and getting drunk with George. We were partying every place we could find in L.A. or New York. It got very, very old.

I was home in Alabama for around five months. Warner Brothers contacted me and wanted to do another album. They told me that this time around, I would be Co-Producer with Jimmy Simpson. I had done a previous album, *Music Speaks Louder than Words*, that didn't do very well. This time, they wanted to record something more disco, so they were ready for the album *Looking for Love*. Songs such as *When You Wake Up Tomorrow, Why Not Rock*, and *Halfway to Heaven* were beautiful songs we were about to record that were sure to receive a lot of airplay.

The next guy to come into my life I met during one of the recording sessions. John Sussewell was my drummer. I thought that he was a very interesting man. I was free from Jimmy James for three years, so I was ready for another relationship. John seemed different than all the other guys that I had dated up to that point. He was very educated, and I was attracted to good-looking educated men. I love men that can make sensible conversations. I like guys that I can enjoy talking with. I am an open person, and I like to talk about things important to me that the man I'm conversing with will understand and relate. I like talking about anything and everything.

I can master most subject matters; even though, I didn't graduate from college. I have learned a lot just from being around educated people. John spoke like an attorney. He had gone to Harvard University, and he had tutored Robert Kennedy's son. He went to Milton Academy in Connecticut, and he played with people like Bill Withers and with Ashford and Simpson on many of their records. He was a drummer for Diana Ross when she recorded her hit song, *The Boss*.

John was on the road with Ashford and Simpson a lot. He was their regular drummer. He was also a number three-called drummer in New York, and I thought it was a blessing to get him because we were looking for a guy with a hard bass drum beat. Jimmy Simpson mentioned him and said if I could afford him, I should hire John Sussewell. With a pedigree like John and Jimmy's recommendation, it was enough for me.

I had John's number in my file, so I called him. He was available, so he came to see me. He was rather aloof when I tried to talk to him while he was setting up his drums. He had very little to say but after the session was over, he asked me if I wanted to have a drink with him. I said, "Yes," and that is how we met.

John opened up a little and talked about himself while we were drinking cocktails. He showed up on time or early every day until we finished recording the record. While I was in New York, we went to movies and concerts. We enjoyed having a few dinners together. We got to know each other and became friends.

I left New York and went back home. One day, John called me. We were both lonely, so I asked him if he wanted to come down to Alabama and visit with me. He was living with his mother at the time, and they were having constant disagreements. He needed to get away for a while. I told him to let me know when he could come, and I would pick him up at the airport.

I did meet John at the airport, and it was great seeing him again. I really liked him, and we had so much fun together. He seemed to like being in the country and especially our house and its location. He said it was therapy for him. I didn't understand fully what John meant by "therapy," and his need for it.

I didn't find out until later that he was a cocaine addict. He was so intelligent and such a businessman. I knew we could succeed together because he was the kind man I had hoped for. I am the kind of woman who loves to set goals and succeed with them. I thought John was more different than any man I had ever been involved with up until I met him. I was wrong again. He was fine as long as we were in the country, but when we went to the city, the desire for drugs triggered within him.

I invited John for a visit, and little did I know that his intentions were to stay. He talked me into letting him put a good band together, so the show would be the best I'd ever done. I knew he was capable of it because he had played with some of the baddest bands on the road.

We had a gig to play at the Village Gate in New York. It was during that time that I became aware of how terrible his addiction really was. We had been together for about a year traveling with my sons, Marcel and Marcus. Marcel played the bass and Marcus, who normally is the drummer, played the percussions because John was on the drums.

We went back to New York for the first time since John left to come to Alabama. We arrived and checked into the hotel that was near many shops on 7th Avenue. John said that he needed new drumsticks. He was carrying travel money that we called "float" money. We used that money to buy gas, and whatever we needed for hotels and other expenses.

We waited for John until the last minute, but he didn't come back to get us at the hotel. We had to do the Village Gate without him, and Marcus played the drums. We had to spend excess money to get taxis to and from the Village Gate because John took the keys to the bus with him.

John's binge lasted three days. He had fun, but so did we. My sons were playing with me. Marcel on the bass and Marcus on the drums. Those boys can play, so the audience loved it. I didn't miss John at all, and I hated it when he came back.

"You need to stay here with your mother, and do what you've always done. We're going home." I told him in no uncertain terms.

John's mother came over and tried to explain his problem. *What problem,* I was thinking. I was so angry I couldn't see straight. He cried for forgiveness and asked me while down on his knees to forgive him. Honestly, I had it with sick and selfish men dumping their problems and dysfunction on the kids and me. I was sick and tired of it.

"If I stay here, I'll die," he begged. "If I stay here in New York, I know I will die."

"Baby, you will just have to die because I'm going home." I told him straight up

John began apologizing to the boys and members of the band, so they convinced me to give him another chance because after all, he did make the band sound very, very good. He was also a great record producer. He's an expert in music, and we had the best band we'd ever had. I gave up and gave in after the band members pleaded his case for him. Understand that when you have been intimate with someone, you tend to soften your heart and have a more sympathetic ear than you normally would have.

I let John come back in the door, and he was very good. Whatever he did while on his romp across New York, he kept a secret. We had some rocky times, but all relationships have rocky times. Within two years, he knew he wasn't going to go back to New York. He asked me to marry him at least fifteen times, and I turned him down every time.

John and I began getting along really well, and I was convinced he wasn't going anywhere unless I kicked him out. I decided to go ahead and marry him. The kids had gotten used to him, and I no longer wanted to live in the state we were in around my children. My youngest son was nine years old now, and I didn't want to have that kind of relationship any longer in my house.

I have the upbringing of my mother, and the Christian inside of me dictated my thoughts. The Scriptures were getting to me about how you should commit this and commit that. You shouldn't commit adultery and fornication, and I was feeling guilty living with John as though we were married, and my children knew we weren't married. I relented and told John I would give it a try. In the back of my mind, I knew we could always divorce. That was my mentality. If it doesn't work, get a divorce. That is exactly how divorces keep increasing every year in our Nation. Divorce has become the alternative to the stresses of working things out.

John started going with me when I was doing disco shows. This happened the first year of our marriage. He would go in our room and get my money, and then trade it for cocaine. When I discovered the money missing, I would have to call the Paragon Agency in Macon, Georgia. Roger Redding was still my booking agent, so I would tell him to send money, so I could get out of the hotel. I couldn't take John with me any longer, so I stopped him from traveling with me to my shows.

John and I began watching Christian television programs. We made it a daily ritual to watch certain shows. We started reading the Bible and when we were reading through the *Book of Revelations*, we couldn't figure out what the meaning was, and it scared the daylights out of us. If you start reading the Bible, read the *Book of John* first and not the *Book of Revelations* until you can find somebody to help you understand it. The *Book of John* is the "love of God" book.

Little by little, we were cleaning up our way of thinking. We read the Bible together in bed first thing in the morning. I was still drinking heavily, and he was smoking weed. *Revelations* amplified everything we were doing. I look back now, and it seems so funny how our desires were changing. I told John that I was going to draw up a contract that would say that if he ever touched cocaine again, he would give me an uncontested divorce. He signed it, and I filed it away.

I decided we were going to move to Birmingham, Alabama. I sold our home in the Colony to be closer to our friends when they came to Birmingham. We actually tired of living in the country although I never thought that would happen. We put our house up for sale. The older boys went to live temporarily with their dad. Terry had enlisted in the Navy. Marcel and Marcus put a band together and were making their own way. A local schoolteacher bought our house.

John and I found a three - bedroom apartment in Birmingham. Cassandra was a senior in high school, and Clarence, Jr. was in the eighth grade. We enrolled them in school, and every body was happy to be living in the big city.

There came a night that changed the direction of our lives. John and I were invited to a local club by one of our friends. The band was playing, the dance floor was crowded, and John had disappeared. I searched all over the place trying to locate him and when I couldn't find him, I returned to our table. John soon appeared and sat down. I asked him if he was ready to leave, and he told me he was.

When we got home, I went to bed, but John didn't come with me. I was too tired to wait for him, so I fell asleep. I woke up about four o'clock in the morning, and I heard John in the kitchen. I tiptoed into the kitchen and caught him snorting cocaine. I went totally berserk. I jumped all over him. I was done. John tried to convince me he wasn't snorting cocaine, but it was obvious. Cocaine was all over the table, and a straw was lying on the table. I told John enough was enough, and I was finished with the marriage.

I went back to bed, and John came into the bedroom.

"Can we talk? He said.

"There's nothing to talk about," I told him as I was pulling out the contract he had signed concerning his cocaine use and divorce. "Here, do you remember when you signed this?"

"I don't know why I do these things," he said as he was begging and pleading. "I don't know why I do them. I really don't blame you."

As soon as it was time for people to be at work, I contacted an attorney whose number I had kept from meeting with him before about divorce. I had already filled in some paperwork, and he told me to come on over that he would meet with me.

John and I started to visit a church on Sundays called Huffman Assembly. Dan Ronisvalle was the Pastor. We thoroughly enjoyed the services, and I could wear make-up and pants. The people were so nice to us, and there was nothing traditional about them as I was used to in the churches I belonged to through the years. They had a children's church, and Junior attended it. We worshipped regularly.

The Word of God was becoming more prevalent to us. It was being explained where we could grow under the teaching and preaching. Some misgivings I had about God began to come clear to me. I had been involved in so many religions that I became hard hearted against religion. I was not about to be conned again. On the other hand, John was all into what was being taught. It was new to him.

I called my son Marcus to take me to see the attorney I had contacted earlier. Marcus came over, and I was in the bedroom dressed and about to walk out. There was a mirror on the wall by the door of the apartment as you go out. I looked in the mirror, and I heard a voice. It was the same voice that told me not to run because my ex-husband couldn't hurt me. I was being protected so don't be afraid.

The voice told me to look at John. I looked behind me, and I had no intentions of saying anything, but the words just popped out.

"Do you need some help?" I asked.

"Yes," John said. "I'll do anything. I'm so tired of this lifestyle and this addiction."

"Call the church we've been attending, and see if you can get some counseling."

"I'll do it Candi if you will go with me."

Marcus was looking at me strange and confused as if to say, "Are you going to do this or not? Make up your mind."

We went to the attorney and filled out the paperwork for the divorce.

Marcus and I arrived at the apartment after meeting with the lawyer. John was still where I left him; sitting in a chair in the bedroom crying. I milled around the house, and his silence was driving me nuts.

"Were you serious about seeing a counselor?" I asked him.

"Yes, I am," he answered."

"Here, call this number if you really are sincere." He had saved the church program from the last Sunday, and the contact information if you needed counseling was on the bulletin.

John called the number immediately, and the secretary answered. He made an appointment for later in the day. I promised John I would go with him, and as soon as we walked out of the apartment, I knew that somehow God was at work.

Pastor Ed O'Neil met with us. He was an older gentleman that had alcohol problems before he was converted to Christ. He knew everything there was to know about dealing with addictions.

Brother Ed handled John very professionally, and at the same time he demonstrated his love and compassion for a person under the enemy that controlled him. I was so impressed and surprised.

John told Brother Ed every secret he was holding inside of himself as he openly wept. He revealed the masturbation habit caused by the addiction. I was dumbfounded because those were things coming out that he had never discussed with me or anyone else.

I wanted help for John because I knew he needed it, but I felt there was nothing wrong with me, and I was okay. I stopped drinking and was taking care of my addiction myself. I was there with John because I wanted to support him as a friend. I had no intention of canceling the divorce. Being there with John was enough, but God had greater plans for our future.

I was in the throes of a new beginning and a different lifestyle was changing my direction. It was a three hundred and sixty degree turn for both of us. What I didn't know was that the best times in my life hadn't happened yet. I had no clue how my steps were being orchestrated by somebody bigger than me. All my life I had asked

God the question, "Why am I here? What is the purpose of my life?" I was about to find out.

I was so stubborn. I was so hurt by church people, and abused by misguided ministers that never searched the Bible deeply enough to rightly divide the Word of Truth. A lot of people like me blame God for their mistakes. It was God's fault that I was abused and misused. I blamed Him for my bad choices.

Of course all that happened to me was not God's doing. I had the freewill to make my own choices, and I was listening to the wrong voice in my ear. The Devil had my attention. I was so mixed up and confused. I heard nothing in the churches I attended except rules, regulations, judgment, and condemnation. I didn't hear about a loving, kind, and forgiving Savior. I was about to meet Him, and He would change my life forever.

John was saved and set free from drug addiction that very afternoon, and I had no doubts that he was truly changed. Something wonderful had happened to him, and I craved that same joy he had found. However, I was so stuck in my career, and I knew if stopped working what would happen. My entire family depended on my income, so that was out of the question.

Two weeks after John's conversion, I was scheduled to make another tour. I was ready to begin my rehearsals, yet my mind was restless, and my heart was confused not knowing what to do. I could hear God calling me. I heard Scriptures that I thought that I had forgotten from my childhood.

God so loved the world that he gave his only begotten Son that whosoever believeth in him should not perish but have everlasting life. John 3:16.

Come unto me all ye that labor and are heavy laden, and I will give you rest. Matthew 11:28

I tried to ignore His voice, and I thought I was going mad, but the thoughts kept coming. John was baptized. I was going to church with him and sitting in the back row of the Sanctuary. I was not about to become a slave to religion and be broke, oh no, I was never going to be broke again.

On Thursday nights, we were supposed to go to Prayer Meeting, but this particular Thursday, I had the urge to go shopping. I don't even remember what I needed to buy.

I was on my way driving on Damascus Road. I was about to make a left turn into a store parking lot, and a Jew driving a Subaru broadsided me. He hit me so hard it turned my truck all the way around. The impact knocked me from under the steering wheel to the other side of the truck. I ended up on my knees behind the captain's chair calling on Jesus to help me.

The van slowly coasted down the road out of the way of the traffic. I was able to work myself from behind the Captain's chair and realized I was still moving down the road. I jumped into the driver's seat, slammed on the brakes, and stopped the car. God protected me.

The police came and wrote up the accident report. I sat dazed as John and my sons took over. I couldn't sleep that night because I was reliving the accident over and over in my mind. I can't explain how restless and confused I was in this valley of decision. I was in that whole wreck. I could hear the noises of the crash, and the impact throwing me around. I had to get up and go to the couch, so I wouldn't disturb John.

God woke me up. He spoke to me and directed me to pick up my Bible. He wanted me to read the entire Chapter of Isaiah 42, and so I said "yes" to the Lord that night. I cancelled my tour and joined Huffman Assembly Church in Birmingham, Alabama the next Sunday.

I called my record label and cancelled my contract, and then cancelled my booking agency, Universal Attractions, in New York City.

Now what? I was thinking. *Have you lost your freaking mind? What are you thinking? Now what?*

I heard another voice say, *Walk by faith and not by sight.* This was the beginning of my faith walk. For twenty-five years, John and I started on our journey. God gave us our own record label, which is called Beracah Records and Beracah Ministries. He gave us two publishing companies, Beracah Publishing and Jemarco Publishing. I cut my first Gospel record in 1983. I was involved with Bible study learning the Word from the Book of Genesis to the Bible Maps.

The first three years we didn't want for anything. We didn't have much money, but we had enough to sustain us.

Jim Bakker was the first to invite us to minister on his PTL network show. He introduced me to a new relationship with Christ. I never knew you could have a relationship with Christ without limits and restrictions, but you can. I hosted two television shows for TBN. The first one was called *New Direction,* and it lasted for ten years. It was replaced by another show called *Say Yes* that ran for twelve years.

I booked many artists on those shows. People like Mary Mary, Kirk Franklin, Yolanda Adams, Dorinda Clark. Lou Rawls was my co-host for thirty-seven shows. I interviewed Karen Clark, Kirk Waylan, Bernice King, Xerona Clayton, Mighty Clouds of Joy, and Deniece Williams. Pastors and evangelists were regular guests. Athletes came on like CeCe Winans, BeBe Winans, and this is the tip of the iceberg. I wish I had space to name them all.

The format was simple. We specialized in testimonies that made the shows so interesting. We were in the top twenty of the best programming on television for twenty-five years. All good things eventually come to an end, and we were finished in the 2,000's. It was very good for me. I was enriched and fulfilled, and we were also pastoring a church with my husband called, Upon this Rock Family Church.

.

CHAPTER EIGHTEEN
He's No Farther Than a Thought Away

We worked hard in those days running the church and traveling and singing. We were ministering in different churches. John stayed clean for ten years as far as I know. The church was growing, and we were growing farther apart. It seemed we were in competition with each other.

John finally got the main stage as the Pastor, and he often let the congregation know that he was running the show. He announced one Sunday,

"If you come into this church to hear Candi Staton, you will be entirely disappointed. I hope you came to see God. That was one hint, and there were more and more hints coming from the pulpit. He started the church while I was on the road. He mentioned to me that he was going to start the church, and I tried to get him to wait for another week, but he was determined to start the church without my presence there.

John didn't wait for me. He put a board together if you could call it a board, and he began the services. He became another control freak as far as I was concerned. Sometimes he would let me teach on Sunday or Wednesday nights. He did most of the preaching, and I was made to understand that I was not the co-Pastor of the church.

We had found a little building after meeting in our hotel for about a year. We took a second mortgage on our house to remodel a leased piece of property against my will. The building was far too large for our small congregation, and the monthly lease was too much for our small congregation to meet the payment every month. We only ministered to about thirty people at the time, and John was spending some of the money on his personal needs or wants.

It took a few months for the church to grow to about one hundred thirty members. We were growing in spite of all the stupidity and to add insult to injury, John's mother moved down to Atlanta. She sold her home in New York and bought property, so she could help us "run the church." She retired from education, and she had more degrees than a thermometer.

"I don't want my mother here," John told me one day. "I don't want her living here."

I didn't understand what he meant then, but I do now. She waltzed in and took control of John, and she tried to control me, but when she found out she couldn't accomplish it, she back stabbed and set up a lot of animosity against me. She began Bible classes in her home. A divisive spirit could be felt entering our church. The sweet spirit that we had slowly died, and the people began to leave. By her second year with us, we had dropped to thirty people again.

John's mother was talking bad about me. She really wanted to be the First Lady of the church. She was talking about me to John. We were so far apart that we were breaking apart little by little. Our marriage was amazingly crumbling. I moved out of the master bedroom into another bedroom in the house and slept in there for seven years. We stayed together, we lived together, but we lived separate lives for seventeen years.

John stayed for long hours in his office. He would come home after whatever he was doing and park in the office at home until daybreak. He was watching porn and masturbating. He had a camera on his computer, so that he could join into live porn groups. He completely quit helping me. My children helped run the record company. He had turned the record label and the publishing companies over to my son and daughter, while he refused to work. He did nothing including paying the bills. John has testified many times on Christian television and in churches across the country.

It was spring break, so I took a vacation with my kids to Pensacola, Florida. I was invited to have dinner with Pastors David and Vernette Rosiers. I hadn't seen them for a long time, but I felt comfortable with them as if we had been in touch every day.

I decided to mention my home situation. I had sought counseling before from bishops and pastors, but their advice was always to stay and pray. I tried that for years and if you only have one person praying, and the other person doing his own thing, you don't get very far. It takes both partners desiring the same things to get results.

These pastors were also prophets. We had been friends for years. When I first began with *Say Yes* on TBN, I often attended their church.

"Candi, you got to leave that house." Bernette told me suddenly. "As soon as you get home, leave that house. I hear glass breaking. He is going to get physical with you. Leave the house."

I had sought real time Christian counseling. After telling my counselor my story, she asked me,

"Can you get him to come to the next session with you?"

"I will try," I replied.

I was so tired of divorces that I would have done anything not to have another one. I approached John and asked him to the next session with me.

"I don't need counseling, you do," he said as he flatly refused.

I went to counseling alone, and my counselor explained why John didn't come with me:

"I knew John wouldn't come," she said. "He has a love/hate for women, and it stems from his childhood, so my advice is to leave him. By the way, I have never told anyone to leave a husband. I don't do that, but I'm telling you, he will never change."

Because of the people in our congregation that believed in John and me, I stuck it out for their sake.

The Rosiers told me to leave my husband. My counselor told me to leave my husband, but I was taking my time. I was tired of leaving and starting over. An opportunity came up through a local radio station that wanted to do a cruise with me. At the time, I had a platform with TBN so I started advertising.

This particular gig was on a cruise ship. The radio station and Candi Staton doing a cruise together gave me a platform, and I started advertising on the radio and telling people where they could get my number if they wanted to book with us and cruise with me.

Two hundred fifty people paid their deposits to go with us. John naturally took over. I couldn't do anything without him, of course. His mother was regularly talking against me, and that helped John and I become eons apart. We almost hated each other at this point. He kept trying to organize the cruise and pull it together.

I went to visit my youngest son on Friday night. My granddaughter, Canzie, begged me to take her home with me. She was about nine years old then. I kept telling her no as she was begging me to stay home. She kept pressing me to let her spend the night with me, and so I gave in and took her home with me.

When I got to the house, John jumped all over me for bringing her home with me without his permission. He was mean. He could be so mean, cold, and selfish.

"Look, John, This is my granddaughter, and this is my house. I live here too, and I don't need your permission to bring my granddaughter home with me. You need to get over it."

The next morning, John was getting ready when he casually announced,

"Oh, by the way, I canceled the cruise."

"No you didn't," I replied. "You have no right to do that."

He rushed at me and put his hands around my throat and pushed me on the bed. He got on top of me with his hands around my throat, and began choking me. When I could breathe, I screamed out a little, and Canzie came running up the stairs screaming.

"Grandma," she yelled. "Stop it, stop it."

John acted as though he had become another person zoned out in another world. He loosened his grip and pulled away from me. He did not delay getting to his car and speeding away.

I was still packed from my trip to Florida. I gathered some more clothes, personal items, check book, important papers, got into my Rav4 Toyota, and drove to my daughter's home. I put everything I could ever use in my car. This was sounding so familiar like the first time I left my husband. *So here we go again,* I thought. I drove to my daughter's house, and I never went back to our house again.

Three weeks went past. John figured out that I wasn't coming home, and I wasn't paying the bills.

"When are you coming home?" John asked me when he called me.

"Never," I replied stiffly. "I'm never going to live with you again. Get used to it. I'm done. I've put up with all I'm going to take from you."

John continued to call and cry. An often too familiar scene with him.

"I'll go to counseling if you'll come home. I'll go to counseling, please come home. I'll do anything you ask me to do."

John's mother called pleading his case. "You know this is wrong. You know y'all got too much going for you. You got the church, you've got lots of stuff going for you."

"You know what?" I practically cussed her out. I called her every witch I could think of. "You're a home wrecking witch. You can have your son back. You got him back now. Be happy. Now, you can be the First Lady when I am out of here."

I stayed in the basement of my daughter's house for nine months, and I was having a home built near my daughter and her husband, Calvin. While I was in the basement, I started writing songs. I wrote one song after another. The basement had no windows, so I was like in my own world for nine months, and I would go over to see how the house was progressing.

When it was finished, I closed on it and moved in. I was divorced from John on March 12th, 1999. I had my ministry, the record company, the publishing company, and I gave John the house and all the furniture because the house had a second mortgage, and he would not be able to pull both mortgages by himself.

John kept the house for possibly two months, and then he sold it. He got nothing out of it, and he didn't deserve anything.

I remained single in my new house for thirteen years. I continued to be active on TBN because Jan and Paul Crouch kept me working. They never like John. Jan was glad he was gone.

"I'm glad you left John," Jan said one day while we were in the bathroom. " I never like him. Paul and I never liked him, anyway."

Paul and Jan kept me on the show for quite some time. I would be there as long as the churches, pastors, and bishops were still watching me on the air. After the word got around that I was divorced, there were still a host of churches that kept me coming to special events. I continued to record Gospel records, and I continued to do my show, *Say Yes*.

Not every pastor was happy about my divorce. They refused to have me because I was divorced. I don't understand why divorce is such a bad nasty thing. Sometimes I think you can kill somebody and get more favor and restoration than you can if you get divorced. Things are changing a little more today.

Pastors rejecting me said they couldn't have the type of woman I was speaking to their precious congregations. Some of the very ones who shunned me, talked about me, and refused to let me in their churches are now divorced. You will reap what you sow.

It was in early 2000 that TBN cancelled my show, and I was no longer visible. All the bookings stopped coming, and everything came to a screeching halt. I was single and jobless. My savings was dwindling away, and I had just recorded my twelfth Gospel album. We were looking for distribution, and we finally found a company in Nashville willing to take my music. I was so excited. I could see the light at the end of the tunnel, and this time it wasn't a train.

I was planning my strategy thinking in terms of promotions, radio and television interviews, and the entire package was going along with releasing new material. Bill Carpenter was my publicist, and he worked with my company doing all the necessary negotiations. We waited and we waited.

I was anxious to find out what was going on, so I called Bill Carpenter.

"Why is this taking so long, Bill?"

I didn't know how to tell you this, Candi," he said. "I don't know what to say except the president of the distribution company called me and said that he doesn't want a divorced woman on his roster."

I hung up the phone. I sat down on the stairs. I screamed at the top of my voice. I cried for two hours. I was so, so church hurt and so disappointed. I couldn't have felt more let down and left out. This was the last straw.

"God," I said to Him when I felt like talking. "I don't care where the doors open, but you've got to help me. Open up any door you want me to go through, and I'll walk through it. I'll walk through any door that you open.

"I got a tour in Europe, will you take it?" Bill said two weeks later when he called.

I didn't hesitate or pray about my answer. I told him to book the tour. I no longer cared if it was a secular tour. I was going on the road in Europe.

I can't thank God enough. He took me off the small stage and put me on the world stage. How awesome is that? The fans in Europe opened their arms to me, and I walked in countries full of pure love. They have shown me so much love. I get leaky eyes whenever I think about it.

The Scripture says the world is God's, and all those that dwell therein. I found out just how big this world is. The people of this world are wonderful, and I shudder to think what I would have done if this tour to Europe hadn't come into my life. The Europeans that are reading this book: please remember how much I love you. Thanks to all my European fans for loving me as well and for not letting my music fade away.

I can forever be thankful to Jules for the booking agency. They are now UA, and I thank him for believing in me and taking me to every level he chose for me to work. I will be forever grateful.

2016 is the fortieth anniversary of *Young Hearts Run Free.* The BBC has never stopped playing my song in all these years. They love that song. *You've Got the Love* went double platinum in Europe. I can't count the times the song has been remixed. I have done many festivals over there. I love them, and I love performing on them.

Europe has a historical way of honoring their music artists that is different than in Europe. They aren't like they are here in America. In America, you are as big as your last hit record. There is an audio legacy in Europe from the first album to the latest CD. It isn't like that here in America.

I am an American, and I love America, but everyone in music is not important in this country. The Europeans know the legacy of a song. They know who played the music behind the vocal background singers, and everyone is important to them. Those of us who have paved the way and stood the storms through segregation, Chiltlin Circuit, and financial hardships to keep our music alive get no credit for our sacrifice and hard work. Nobody wants to pay us what we're worth, and we're still no better than our last record. It is one of the reasons that so many artists have moved to Europe and make those countries their home. It is because of the extraordinary care they receive.

The UK is so special to me. I love London, and I love the BBC. It is so amazing how they've been to me, and I love and appreciate them. I've been blessed to travel the world. I've been active in the UK and Europe for twelve years or more. I've been to Ireland, Scotland, Australia, Austria, Holland, and Paris, France many times. So many countries I've been to.

I have a lovely band that's worked with me. Ernie McCone is on bass, and he is our bandleader. Mark Vanderhoof, Mick Talbot is on the keyboards, my son, Marcus Williams is my drummer. Crispin Taylor used to play the drums. Suzie Furlonger and Xavier Barnett are my background singers and have been with me ever since we started, and I call them my UK family. We have so much fun together. We traveled to many shows, and it was uncanny that when I first met them that they knew every song I'd ever sung.

We walked into the rehearsal hall, and I was unsure about the band. I had an uneasy feeling whether they would fit my music. When they started playing, I was overjoyed with excitement. They sounded just like my records. They have been with me now for twelve years, and every time I go to rehearse with them, I am so glad to see them because we've had so many wonderful experiences together. They are wonderful people, and I love them so much.

I am proud to say that I've been blessed to have come this far and survived all the drama. I had to endure, but I had good times also. I know I am a survivor.

I would like to take time here to share a few things before I go on with my story. I guess you noticed that I've several divorces. It's common, but it's traumatic. Divorce is hurtful, and it's a Devilish things. I don't know how I've gone through so many of them, but I did.

What is divorce really like? It's like tearing apart two hearts that once held love. Verbal abuse replaces the communication that once held you together. Talking to each other becomes unbearable. The children are affected, and the entire family suffers. What may have been a close knit and fun loving family are now strangers or even enemies in their own home.

Family members take sides. The division of property is horrendous. You worked so hard to build your lives and buy a home, and now it is torn into pieces. You think you are losing your mind. You don't want to go through it, but you have no choice. It's too painful to stay with someone who seems to hate you, and you hate that person.

The end comes, and now the marriage is done. There are no mutual agreements anymore like a marriage partnership should have. There is no hope of reconciliation because it's time to move on.

I was so tired of getting to this place in marriage. I can't ever go through another one again. How devastating a divorce can be. I wish everyone who takes marriage vows could stay together, but unfortunately that is not realistic.

I heard Dr. Phil make a statement on *The View*.

"I will never write a tell all book about my failed relationships or ex wives. I just won't do it."

I agree with him to a certain extent in the sense that if you are telling your story for revenge in order to get back at somebody, it is wrong if that is your motive. If your intention is to help someone make better decisions and choices by reading your story, then I believe a tell all book is worth writing. I wish more people had written books that had gone through what I've gone through. You could have shed more light on my path and allowed me to see red flags before I ran into them in my own sordid relationships. What a blessing that would have been for me.

There are so many songs left unsung, and too many books left unread. There are cures for diseases lying in the graveyards today. I still retain my sanity because of a book that I carried with me as I went through my storms in life. It is *The Verbally Abusive Relationship, How to Recognize It, and How to Respond* by Patricia Evans. I carried the book in my purse on planes for years. It gave me the courage I needed to let go of bad relationships. I realized I was being abused. Patricia taught me to recognize the abused woman syndrome. I didn't even know what that was. I didn't know there was such a syndrome. How verbal abuse leads to physical abuse is just a matter of time. That's why I got away from the abuse and didn't murder my abusers.

I had the courage to leave those bad marriages. The book taught me how to recognize "crazy-making," ever increasing confusion to throw you off track. It explained how two people could live in two different realities in the same house and when you express yourself, it's always rationalized as if it doesn't matter. Our feelings always matter.

What if Patricia Evans had not written that book? I thank you, Patricia for pouring your heart into your book. It really helped me because when you've been born and raised in an abusive environment, abuse seems normal to you. There is nothing normal about abuse. Learn to command respect and don't tolerate any kind of abuse whether it is verbal, physical, or otherwise.

CHAPTER NINETEEN

I'd Rather Be an Old Man's Sweetheart Than to Be a Young Man's Fool

It's 3:00 a.m., and the texts and emails kept coming over and over again. The familiar beeps everyone is familiar with from smart phones and computers. He gets tired of it, but he answers them. This had become normal for me night after night for four months. It would get worse and more frequent about 1:30 a.m. Sometimes, it went on constantly until 5:00 a.m.

I used to have to wear earplugs, so I could get some sleep. This irritation would invade my bedroom night after night until he got tired and silenced his phone. When I questioned him about why he had to keep answering those calls, he said that he couldn't turn his phone off.

He explained that it might be the guys from the *On Track Recovery* program. This was a ministry that provided housing facilities for drug addicts and convicted felons who were still incarcerated because they had no address to be released to. I didn't believe him. I knew those calls were from strip clubs, and other women he was involved with.

One night, the texting and beeping kept coming as usual. I had it up to my ears. It was enough. This particular night, I was not in any mood to take it. The phone kept ringing and beeping, and obviously he was supposed to meet somebody but failed to show up, and she was livid.

I was trying to sleep. I tried everything I could to ignore those beeps, but she kept calling, and he finally answered the phone. I could hear this loud, angry female screaming obscenities at him.

"You better tell that trick not to call my house and waking me up. You better control your 'ho's," I said to him after I couldn't stand it anymore.

He hung up the phone, threw me over, and straddled my body. He sat on me, put the palms of his hands on my chest and drew his fist back to hit me. I pushed his hands away and started taunting him.

"Oh, you bad, bad boy, huh? So you're gonna hit me because your 'ho called you and woke me up? How dare you, you lowdown dirty, sick, twisted, lying fool. You better get off me now. I dare you to hit me. I have four grown sons that will hunt you down until you're dead."

He got up. I turned on the lights. He was standing over me shaking with anger and rage with his fist still balled up to hit me. He then proceeded to manhandle me, and he pushed me into the wall still shaking. I knew he wanted to knock me down and step on me, but I am sure he thought about what I said. I pushed him and left the room.

I should have called 911, but I didn't. I went to the guest room. I was totally shaken at what had taken place. He never apologized, and I don't think he ever will for all he did to me. In my whole life, I have never met anyone so arrogant, evil, and cold.

He didn't say he was sorry because he wasn't. This was normal behavior for Otis Nixon. Cheating and lying were normal for him. I told him when we first got together that I was aware that I was older than him.

"If you ever want to be free," I began my lecture. "You won't have any problems from me. You're free to go, and I'll give you my blessings but when you cheat, you're always living in fear of getting caught. I know how a person acts that cheats. I've been through a bunch of cheating relationships. I don't know what causes it; maybe it's the thrill of how much you can get away with without getting caught. I've experienced this so many times. I know that a guilty conscience produces fear, and fear is anger turned inside out."

This man knew when he married me that he had no plans to be faithful to me. He saw an opportunity and jumped on it. I can't judge him now because I hope he's changed. I really pray for him all the time. I pray that he will change.

It was never in Otis to be truthful, loyal, or moral. He had no intentions, had no respect because that's who he was. When he was high on crack, he was worse. He would become very cruel, uncontrollable, and no feelings for anyone but himself, and a desire to find more drugs. He was a driven man. I have pity on anyone who is addicted and has no will.

I have a son that got into drugs when he was in the Navy, and I am working with him. He got hooked on Oxycontin, and he has many problems with his body, and he's sick much of the time. I have so much compassion for him because addiction is so difficult to break. I care for Otis even after all he's done to me.

My reason for sharing my story is to warn women old and young about the deception and pain I endured because I was lonely. I was a cougar. I learned, and I learned fast. If you're dating a younger man, make sure he loves you and not for what he can get from you. You are not a ladder for him to climb up to the next level, or on your back to get on his feet.

When I first met Otis, I had no intentions or desire to hook up with him. I was very well established, and I wasn't looking for a man. I wasn't looking for a husband. I owned my own home, and had two fancy cars in the garage. I had been divorced for thirteen years, and I was doing a lot of touring in Europe and the UK. I had a record that went platinum over there. It's called, *You Got the Love*. It has been recorded many times by singers such as Florence and Machine, Josh

Stone, and many others. I was not hurting for money. I had done the Glastonbury Festival twice, and the WOMAD Festival many times.

I do festivals all the time. I am still working in the UK with Earth, Wind, and Fire, Neil Rogers, and Chic. The late great Isaac Hayes, Stevie Wonder, Jay-Z and many other superstars I shared the stage with.

I drew a crowd of fifty thousand people in Glastonbury. I made lots and lots of money, but I am not bragging. I was being blessed. The point is, I was not searching for a man with money.

Otis wasn't doing too well when I met him. He lost a multi-million dollar home that was a mansion. He is famous for his catch for the Atlanta Braves during a playoff game that allowed them to get to the World Series. Otis didn't play in the series. He was arrested for possession of crack cocaine. He was taken into custody as he celebrated his success. He wrote a book called, *Keeping It Real.*

I met Otis and went to his apartment one time. We were working together. He was living then in a two - bedroom apartment and didn't have a car. He had a 25" TV sitting on an apple cart in the living room. His furniture was old and pitiful. He had a small bed and a few clothes in the closet.

I thought Otis Nixon was rich, but this was ridiculous. He kept showing me newspaper clippings of what he used to be and a video of his mansion that used to be. He was confessing how drugs had robbed him of his money, dignity, self-esteem, and he wanted people to know through the book he was writing what drugs will do to you.

Otis swore that he was finished with drugs. Usually when you write a book that you want to help other people, you are closed with that chapter in your life. In Otis's case, he wasn't.

I was so naïve about crack. I was so out of touch with reality about the world of drugs. I knew all about cocaine, and I tried it myself back in the day. I knew about uppers, downers, and alcohol. I dropped all my bad habits in 1982 when I became a Christian. I never touched them again.

I was thinking that Otis had done what I did. He was off the drugs but when I met Otis, people were warning me about him and saying,

"If I can stop my drug and my alcoholism, I believe anybody can change."

Otis told me he had the desire to be a blessing to others that are where he used to be He told me about his passion to open a home for drug addicts and help them get clean, and to allow men that are incarcerated to get out of the jails.

I must admit I was impressed with his resolve, goals, and purpose. My son was incarcerated at one time, and I tried to find a place where I could get his life together. I couldn't find anything or anybody to help him. With Otis, I had the chance to help distressed addicts to straighten out their lives.

I began working with Otis very closely. I helped him edit his book, and I helped him choose his cover. I was his partner to help establish his house to take in inmates that had nowhere to go. I was excited. It was also my passion. We established two houses and allowed inmates to move in. It was wonderful in the process of working so close together. It was wonderful, and he had a great sense of humor.

We started dating, and one thing led to another. I always reminded him that I was a bit too old for him.

"That doesn't matter," he said. "Age is only a number, and you're beautiful. You don't even look your age. I love you, and I want to marry you."

"Otis, you must be joking. I am too old for you. My oldest son is your age. I don't rob the cradle."

Otis kept on being very persuasive, and I knew I would regret it, but I told him I would marry him. He had already moved into my house, and he was already telling me about how it looked to other people. It didn't look right for us living together without being married, and I have children and grandchildren.

Otis was persuasive, and when the flesh is in control, you make the wrong choices. I was tired of being alone, and being with someone refreshing and exciting appealed to me. We had a good time because Otis was so funny. The way he expressed himself would get you caught up in his rhetoric, and he could win you over. Sometimes I knew he was lying, but it was still funny. We stayed busy with meetings and never a dull moment.

On Track was really growing. We were able to have a meeting with Governor Deal. He gave us access to a detention center in Cedartown, Georgia. It would house two hundred men. Each man would get seven hundred dollars a month from the Government. Governor Deal wanted to give us his grant writer, so that we could fund the project. I would be teaching the men and be on salary. I wouldn't have to work on the road unless I wanted to.

We had a board made up of attorneys, a CPA, and several other businessmen and women. We were ready to open. Governor Deal had signed off on this project and was about to make us a model recovery program in more than one state. We were looking at making millions of dollars, but it never came to pass because Otis couldn't stop doing drugs. He relapsed, and my life became a living hell.

Otis was charming during the days we were preparing the On Track program. We put on golf tournaments every year to raise money to keep the house supplied, and we had thirty men in the house. I was teaching on Thursday nights in a home.

On the outside, things were really good. The men in the program were actually growing. Their lives were changing because Otis was a good leader. He knew how to run the ship, and I had never met a person who knew how to deal with these types of people that were drug addicts and inmates. He was doing an excellent job.

We could have made a success of the program if he could have kept his mind on what he was doing. He needed to drop his best friend, who was his drug dealer. Otis kept falling off the wagon, and I tried to keep it hidden to cover him. His friends, family, and others connected to On Track were trying to get him to stop because the noise on the streets was about him and his habit. It was only a matter of time before Governor Deal and his staff would find Otis out.

Otis got worse instead of better. We had so much to lose but as we all know, you have to want a change, or you will never change. He got worse no matter how much I wanted to straighten him out.

We went to Las Vegas to get married. It was eerie, but we went to the Little White Chapel just to look it over. A female pastor was there on duty. She was an ordained minister, and she kept walking back and forth, looking at me with a frown on her face.

"I have a word from the Lord for you," she said to me, and I went with her.

Otis left the room, and she asked me to step into another room with her.

"I don't know you," I said.

"I don't know you, either," She replied. "But God is saying don't do this. You will regret it if you do." She grabbed my hand and prayed for me while Otis walked in.

"What was that about?" He said, and I told him I didn't know.

We married on Otis's birthday, January 9, 2010. We got married in the Little White Chapel in Las Vegas. I want to clear up that the program was already in progress when we got married.

The words the Pastor said to me haunted me all night. Today, I wish I had heeded those words. They were from God, and I knew it. Had I listened, this Chapter would not be in this book.

Two weeks after I married Otis, he started disrespecting me, cursing me out, and calling me names. I hadn't heard that kind of language in twenty-five years. We had moved into a new home, and I had given my house to Marcus, my son, and he let us have his house as an intake home.

I am now stuck in this new house with Otis Nixon. He started in on me the first night in the new house. He cursed me out, and I was literally in shock. I never expected that kind of behavior from him. I met the real Otis Nixon.

You don't really know someone until you live with him. Before you marry, people know how to hide bad behavior until you say, "I do," and then all hell breaks loose. I believe it's because the law has been written long before you and I existed that gave a man the right to own a woman. This has to stop.

CHAPTER TWENTY

When Will I Ever Learn,
All My Worry is a Waste of Time

When will I ever learn, all my worry is a waste of time.
When will I ever learn letting go brings peace of mind.
When will I ever see things have a way of working out'
When will I ever be free, free from fear, free from doubt.
O Lord I pray to You, give me the faith to make it through.
I see the lonely sparrow fly, and I wonder when will I?

By Dan Tyler (Mota Music/Intuit Music Group)

Whatever God didn't build won't last. You can prop yourself up all you want to, but it's still going to fall apart. Someone has a famous name, and everything that shines is not gold. If the person has a famous name and legacy, don't be fooled.

I stayed with Otis about eighteen months, and I'm very surprised it lasted that long. I knew within a month after I married him that I had made one of the worse mistakes in my life. I had thirteen years living alone and had a happy, joyful life. Now, I found myself trapped in the same type relationship that I had gone through with every marriage. It's like an inescapable trap laying wait for me to fall into.

The first Christmas we had together he bought my gifts at a thrift shop and gave them to me. OMG. We went by a thrift shop that a friend of Otis owned. I looked through some racks just wasting time. Otis told me to pick something out. I found a couple of things I liked, and told him that they were cute. I didn't need any clothes.

I have more than enough clothes, but I was in the store, the dresses were cute, I was bored, so I said, "Okay." His friend probably gave them to him.

It was November when we were in the shop. Christmas Day came, and I asked Otis where my gift was. I got him a leather jacket, some shirts, and some cologne.

"You already have your Christmas gifts, remember? Don't you remember the cute little dresses you picked out at the thrift shop?" He responded.

The shop did have some really nice stuff, but you expect more than that from your husband on Christmas. That hurt me, and I knew then that was about the depth of how he really felt about me. I bought him so much that year, and I had nothing under the tree.

The next Christmas, I got no presents from Otis at all. There was nothing for me. He was so sloppy with his cheating. I found condoms in his pants pockets and other places.

In January after New Years, I was going through some check stubs in the office. I found a canceled check he had written to Macy's for six hundred fifty nine dollars. He gave somebody a gift. The name he put on the memo line was "Bouncy." It sounded like a stripper's name to me.

I was so hurt. Otis would go out, get high, and stay gone for days. Each month, his retirement check would come. He had a good pension set up for himself. Three days later, he would be broke, and the burden to pay the bills would fall on me again.

I traded my Lexus and got a Toyota Tundra pickup. Otis used my credit to get it, and he never paid a dime on it. He promised me in the finance office he would make every payment.

"Don't worry," he said. "I got this." The truck was two months behind on payments when they started calling me from collections. I was in London when I got the first call.

When I got back home, I told him that he had to put his money with mine. We had more than enough money to pay all the bills on time with some left over. I paid the electric and the phone bills. Otis had a phone on my account. He had nine dollars and ninety-eight cents to pay each month, and never paid that. He wouldn't pay it, so I told him if he wasn't going to pay for anything to at least pay the house payment. The house payments were always two months behind. He paid it just in time to keep the house out of foreclosure.

My credit was ruined. You better be careful, who you allow in your life. Don't let someone come into your life that you don't know and allow him to destroy everything you're working towards. I don't intend to bore you with my trials and tribulations, but you better know, who you are marrying.

Otis and I lived in a house with seven and a half bathrooms and six bedrooms. We had a beautiful twenty by forty feet pool in the ground on a three - acre lot in the country near Angel Food Ministries. Most of the guys living at On Track worked there, so that's why we counted it a blessing to find a home so close to our work.

Otis invited the board and friends to the house often. It never ceases to amaze me how women can flirt with your husband right in your face. They think that everything in the house belongs to him because he's the breadwinner. They would be surprised to know that he owned nothing. Everything in the house belonged to me and was brought from my old house to the new house.

Otis had a pornographic addiction on top of his other addictions. He was comfortable and got sloppy again. He ordered pornography on my account. Some months the bills to purchase the sites would be as high as three hundred dollars. I had to put a safety lock on my computer and lock him out like a child to keep him off the sites.

"You're a dried up old bitch," he called me. "Your old dried up ass. Shut up before I put my foot up your ass. I don't want you."

"You wanted me before you got me," I said. "Before you got the house and truck, huh? Now you don't want me anymore?"

The last straw for me was when he started making passes at my granddaughter. He would call her and talk all night when he was high. She kept it from me at first because she didn't want to hurt me until it got ridiculous. Her father stepped in and put a stop to Otis ever calling her again.

I moved out of the house and found a wonderful place in a beautiful neighborhood right across from a golf course. My daughter lives in the community. I can't thank God enough for deliverance. God said, *I will prepare a table before you in the presence of your enemies.*

Otis tried to destroy my reputation by started a rumor that I had a boyfriend in the UK. He lied on me. I do go to the UK on tours but never to develop an intimate relationship. It makes no sense because the distance is too far, and it is stupid unless you're going to live there.

Otis said I was dating some guy. I am too busy for this kind of nonsense. When I go to Europe, I work. I work hard every day while on tour. When I'm off, I'm resting. He told several pastors these lies, and they believed him. They were Braves fans, and he had the upper hand. They would believe anything he would say.

Celebrities have faults and weaknesses like everybody else. We need to stop putting stars on pedestals. The media needs to take a timeout because they are making Gods out of celebrities. Music and sports is what we do for a living, it is not who we are. It is what goes on when we're off stage that makes us who we are.

The sports celebrities are the worst. Those characters beat their wives, take drugs, bully people, are disrespectful, rapist, and all they ever get is a slap on the wrist. They get away with all this because managers and team owners can only see dollar signs. Thank God something is beginning to be done with nefarious behavior. The NBA and NFL are punishing their players when their undisciplined behavior puts them in the spotlight.

If these actions remain consistent, these characters won't have a chance to unleash their fury and rage on our family members and us.

Football is such a contact sport, a vicious game that causes a lot of pent up frustrations. I understand all of that. When they get home, they still act out some of the frustrations they've had on the football field, and the spouse becomes a target.

I am planning to start a ministry for battered and abused women. I think it's time for me to do it. God knows we need love and understanding. We're not damaged goods. We are wonderful and special people. We want to be treated that way. Control over another human being is another phase of bullying, whether it is sister, brother, mother, father, wives, husbands, or teammates.

We must show love and compassion for every person on this earth because we don't know their story. Please be kind and don't take kindness for weakness. Women are not weak, but through put down words we hear every day telling us we're not good enough, rich enough, don't have enough sense, strong enough, pretty enough, shapely enough, and too fat or too skinny.

Speak to yourself when you hear this garbage. Tell yourself that you are beautiful and smart. You are fine and have supernatural strength. Remind yourself every day that you can make it. Fifteen minutes a day spend time speaking positive things to you about yourself.

God knows how words hurt, and what it takes to build yourself back to self-respect. People used to say, "Sticks and stones can break my bones, but words will never hurt me."

That's a lie. Words can not only hurt you but also destroy you. Words can destroy your self-esteem, your confidence, and whatever you're trying to build. To counteract these hurtful sayings you hear everyday, stop answering to words you are called that you are not. Stop answering to bitch. You're not a bitch. I don't care what those rappers and others call you, that is not who you are.

I wake every day chanting about who I am for fifteen minutes. I am perfectly whole as God created me to be. Those are good and wonderful words. This habit will build back your self-confidence after it has viciously been torn down.

Otis got restless after he moved in the house and got his truck.

"Why don't you leave," he told me. "I don't want you anymore. Get out of my life."

"Why don't you leave?" I replied back to him. "If you're so unhappy with me, why don't you go? I'm not leaving my home."

"Well, I'm not leaving," he replied.

I started making my plans for escape. I couldn't stay there in that environment and walk on landmines every day. According to Otis, I didn't know how to talk, look, or manage anything in my life practically. I got so frustrated being me, and I thought, *Why is it that every time I get into a relationship, it turns around and ends up exactly like my first relationship. What is on me that needs to come off? What is it that I have not forgiven?*

This is something that I think about every time I get a man in different suit. When will it stop? I don't look for these people, they somehow find me.

I made plans to find another place to live. My daughter-in-law, Tasha, recently got her real estate license, and she called me a week after my confrontation with Otis, and he was on a four day binge.

"Mom, I think I found you a house. Can you come over here right now?" Tasha asked when she called me.

I put my blue jeans on, jumped in my car, and drove over to where Tasha was. I walked into the house and fell in love immediately. I told her I wanted it. She told me there were three other people in front of me that had already signed up, but we should pray about it.

We prayed on the spot, and I filled out the contract for the lease. I wanted a year's lease because I believed that I heard the voice of God say that I would get my house back in the divorce. I would leave Otis for a year, and then move back in my house.

The person I leased the house from was a minister and pastor. He told me when I moved in that he had three contracts in front of him including mine. He said he closed his eyes and asked the Lord to reveal the person that should lease his house. God told him it was the one on the right of him, and it was mine. That's how I got the house. It took a week for me to get approved, and I paid the first and last month's rent and moved.

Otis had an engagement in North Carolina. He was speaking, signing his new book and baseballs. He was supposed to stay over there for two days. I grabbed seventeen people, and we met at the old house. My whole family was there and friends of my sons that were big strong dudes, and we loaded up two trucks. It took five hours to get it all done. We rushed over to my new home and put all the stuff in the house. I stayed with my daughter until the utilities were turned on.

Otis had gone on four-day binges before, and I don't think he thought that I would leave him, but he didn't know me. I would not take any more abuse and take a chance of losing my life.

Otis called me and asked how I was, and to tell me he was on his way home. I told him I was fine, which I was. He was leaving the airport. I know he was buttering me up and trying to smooth things over before he got home. It was too late.

When Otis arrived home and walked into the house, all he saw was an old recliner and the TV on the wall with no cable. If the truck had been big enough, I would have taken that stuff, too.

I would have loved to have been a fly on the wall to see his face when he walked through the door. A couple of hours later, my phone rang.

"Where did you put my blood pressure medicine?" He asked in the softest most polite voice.

Immediately, a song popped into my head. "To the left, to the left, everything you wanted is in a box to the left. You must not know about me. I can have another you in a minute; matter of fact, he'll be here in a minute, baby."

For two months, we were still married. I was only living in the other house. Otis moved a Caucasian girl in the house with him before we were divorced. She moved in with her dog, and they were going to be happy in my house forever. God is always around. He will see you through it all if you trust Him. God told me not to worry because it wasn't going to last.

The house went into foreclosure. I was still living in the leased house near my daughter. I woke one morning and knew immediately something had gone wrong. I called the bank, and they told me that my house would be foreclosed that morning. I asked them if it is too late to do something? I was told they hadn't started the paperwork yet. I asked the banker lady if I could buy my house back, and how much would it cost to get it. She told me I could buy it back, but I needed to be at the bank with a cashier's check by two o'clock that afternoon.

I found the money and rushed to the bank with a cashier's check, and they overrode the foreclosure. My divorce became final on December 12, 2012.

The things we do for love. The price we pay to be with someone; we are not alone. It's so deep it's hard to figure out. When things are going great for you, loneliness sometimes sets in. Al Green's song so smoothly says, "I'm so tired of being alone." You think you've found the one to share your aspirations and dreams with. You find out you got another jerk, another loser to deal with until you get to the point of not even caring if you have the right one or don't.

CHAPTER TWENTY-ONE

His Hands

You can use your hands to do good things or bad things. What would you do without hands? They are necessary because they feed us food to eat, nurture our bodies, nurture our babies, and our loved ones. They can put wood on the fireplace to warm us. They can steer a car in the right direction. They can open a car door. They can keep our bodies warm and clean. They can point us in the right direction, mow our lawns, clean our houses, hold us up, and pick us up. Nearly everything we do includes the use of our hands.

Hands can also be destructive. They can pull the rug from under us. They can cause us to lose our balance. They can take a knife and cut up our food, or they can cut up another person. They can slap us or caress us. They can choke us and abuse us. They can push and shove and throw a stone, and back us up against a wall. Hands can be weapons of mass destruction. Think about our hands. Take a moment to look at your hands. You can use them anyway you want because they're yours and under your control. That's what happens in a relationship.

What does cause abusive relationships? I'm not an expert, but I am an experienced abused person, and it begins when you give your personal power away. We were all equipped with human feelings when we were born. Our feelings are involved with emotions. We know when we are being mistreated, and a small baby is cognizant of that. We have human esteem. We know we're somebody special in our own rights. We have certain rights as human beings. We desire love. We desire nurturing, and feelings of importance. We crave love and affection. This is why so many love songs have been written and continue to be written, and we go out and buy them because we crave and thrive on love. If you can't get the men you love to tell you every day that they love you, buy a CD. Let Peabo Bryson or Luther Vandross or somebody tell you.

Someone had to tell me this. It's like the air I breathe, and the water I drink. I crave it. I'll be anything or do anything just to hear it. To have human contact even if it's negative. Ah, I think I am about to strike a nerve.

When did negative attention begin? Most of the time it starts at home when we were very small children. We had siblings to compete with. How much love can I get from my mama and my dad? It seems like my baby brother and sister get all my parent's attention. So what if the baby spilled the milk, kicked the cat, or messed up the bed by jumping up and down on it? Now I get their attention. So often negative attention starts just like that. Your parents yelled at you. They said you are bad, and they punish you. They say you won't amount to much. I must be the bad seed in the family. You get used to the negative treatment, and somehow you must seem to be drawn to people that treat you badly. You've learned to be completely comfortable in that setting. If you come in contact with people who truly respect you, it's so hard to believe they're sincere. They must want something in return. Surely they are not for real. I know I don't deserve to be treated that kind, that loving. I didn't earn it. I have to do something special to be loved. As a teenager, I had to give them sex in order to be loved. As a child, I had to do something really spectacular to be loved.

I earned everything I got as a child. I sung to be loved. I noticed when that when I sang a song, people loved me. They praised me, they complimented me, they wrote about me and how wonderful I was. The song says when will I find love? Some folks search all their lives and never find the right person that fits like a glove in the hand.

Why do we find ourselves in abusive situations? No matter how subtle it might be, abuse is abuse. There is emotional, physical, and Spiritual abuse. When you allow someone to speak to you in a wrong tone of voice, put you down, call you names, disrespect you, use you for the purpose of brainwashing you into believing they love you and care about you. You're only being set up for further abuse.

All abuse begins verbally. Don't allow anyone to abuse you. You must set standards and boundaries as a life guide and allow no one to step over them. When they call you that first name, and they say you're fat, or call you a bitch, and when you start to set them straight. Right then stop them immediately. People will do whatever you allow them to do. If they insist on being rude to you, drop them and move on. Don't underestimate destructive energy. Destructive energy is dangerous; it's toxic. You will be sucked into abuse.

Physical abuse comes when you allow verbal abuse. You can guarantee physical abuse is moving in. When you don't correct verbal abuse, it will rob your soul of the healthy thoughts of life. Depression stems from unhealthy thoughts rattling in your brain and dominating your thinking. Your mind, will, and emotions are all affected by verbal abuse. Physical scars will eventually heal, but scars on the heart will never heal. You can learn to live with them sometimes through therapy, but they always find a way to pop up.

You may be having the time of your life in a positive setting, feeling good about yourself, and you'll get a pop up. If you're so important, why didn't Jimmy think so? If you're so important, why didn't John think so? You have to quickly answer because he's evil. He was evil and he was terrible, and he kept on having a good time.

At this point, a lot of us retreat into quietness and withdraw.

Physical is just a confrontation of the verbal. He said I was a poor excuse for a woman. He said I was a no good or something. He said I was a poor excuse for a woman. He said I would never amount to anything. He said I was weak and dumb. He told me I was I was ugly and fat. I guess he was right, so I guess I deserve to be beaten, to be kicked, pulled by my hair across the floor. I guess he was right. That is the "poor me" syndrome of an abusive relationship.

One of the kickers is Spiritual abuse. It starts under a Spiritual leader. Some dumb misinformed man of God or woman of God that was abused as a child is going to put that same mistreatment upon you and lie on God. God said you can't wear pants or dress up and look decent.

God said, "Give me all your money." Don't be ignorant in Spiritual things. Learn your rights and principles as a child of God. Be led by the Spirit of God or the sons and daughters of God Don't be led by somebody's craziness. His hands lead you and guide you into all truth. Use God's hands. Keep toxic people out of your inner circle.

We need a good old-fashioned detox. Walking on eggshells anticipating the next episode of trauma. You are not allowed to express your real feelings. You constantly hide. You can never feel safe. Shame, humiliating, inflicting guilt, criticizing, joking, belittling, controlling. discrediting, disproving, inflicting fear, breaking promises, if only you were different or better.

I have the right to say no to anything when I'm not ready. I have a right to dignity and respect. I have a right to make my own decisions, and I have a right to terminate conversations with others that make me feel put down and humiliated. I have a right to all of my feelings. I have a right to change my mind, and I have a right for my own personal space in times that I need to be alone. I have all these rights because I'm a woman.

EPILOGUE

I know this book has been an emotional ride not only for me but for many of you as well. I've cried a little, and I've also laughed at some of the places this winding road of life has carried me. Yet, I have survived.

I would like to end this book on the brighter side of life for me. After my last divorce, I gave up all hope of ever getting married again. I felt I had no more capacity in my heart for marriage or love. Can you blame me? God had blessed me with all the necessities in life that I would ever need. I was done. But in October 2015, I was invited to speak at a women's meeting by Pastor Kenneth Whalum and his wife Sheila. Reverend Whalum is the Pastor of New Olivet Baptist Church in Memphis, Tennessee. I met them through the influence of the late David Gest.

After the service, Pastor Whalum took me by the hand and said, "I want you to meet someone". He is in charge of the security here at our church. His name is Henry Hooper.

I was introduced to Mr. Henry Hooper. He is a tall, dark, and handsome man, who served in the United States Secret Service for four Presidents. President Richard Nixon, President Gerald Ford, President Jimmy Carter, and President Ronald Reagan were his assignments. He also served as a Secret Service Agent to Vice President George W. Bush, Senior while he was in office with President Ronald Reagan.

We exchanged cell phone numbers and began to converse. He also told me about his bout with Mohammad Ali in 1960 at Cow Palace in San Francisco. They were fighting for a spot on the U.S Boxing Team for the Olympic games held in Rome, Italy that year. They were representing the U.S Marines Corps in the qualifying trials. He was also a Green Beret in the U.S. Marine Corp. Today, Henry is the owner of his own State Farm Insurance Agency in Memphis TN.

Needless to say, I was impressed. Henry is the kind of man that I've looked for all my life. When I stopped looking, God sent him. We got married on July 12th 2016. I couldn't be more happy and blessed. I can stop kissing frogs hoping they will turn into a prince. Now, I have a Prince.

So ladies, my advice to you is to be patient, don't get ahead of God, and He will bring the right soul mate into your life.

Sincerely,
Candi Staton

The summation of everything that is in this book, you just read. I hope you've been blessed, and I hope you have an enjoyable and Spirit-filled life. I hope you enjoyed the book and got something out of it. If you did, please send me an email, write a review on Amazon.com, and tell others about the book.

You can order the books at heritagebuilderspubishing.com, Amazon.com, or any bookstore.